That's
a
Rap

That's a Rap

MATTYB

with TRAVIS THRASHER

G

GALLERY BOOKS

NEW YORK   LONDON   TORONTO   SYDNEY   NEW DELHI

G

Gallery Books
An Imprint of Simon & Schuster, Inc.
1230 Avenue of the Americas
New York, NY 10020

First Gallery Books hardcover edition June 2016

GALLERY BOOKS and colophon are registered trademarks of Simon & Schuster, Inc.

For information about special discounts for bulk purchases,
please contact Simon & Schuster Special Sales at 1-866-506-1949
or business@simonandschuster.com.

The Simon & Schuster Speakers Bureau can bring authors to your live event.
For more information or to book an event, contact the Simon & Schuster Speakers Bureau at 1-866-248-3049 or visit our website at www.simonspeakers.com.

Interior design by Davina Mock-Maniscalco

Manufactured in the United States of America

10   9   8   7   6   5   4   3   2   1

Library of Congress Cataloging-in-Publication Data is available.

ISBN 978-1-5011-3379-4
ISBN 978-1-5011-3382-4 (ebook)

Introduction

The coolest thing in the world is finding something that's rare. Something that might look like everything else, but it is absolutely one of a kind. It could be a baseball card or a limited-edition sneaker or a signed flyer or a snapshot. It could be anything. The value doesn't come from some price tag put on it. It comes from being totally unique.

Over the years, I've collected all kinds of rare things. I have several favorite hats that sit on my desk in my room. A stack of autographs from different famous people I've met; my multicolored

special-edition Nike KDs that I got online. Special pins and mementos, pieces of art I've made.

But none of that compares to something that's even cooler, which is the fact that every one of us is a unique person.

It's easy to say that if you're someone like my sister, Sarah Grace. She's the youngest in our family and the only girl (with four brothers!). She's funny and feisty and cute, and she was born with Down syndrome. She definitely is one of a kind.

People say that about someone like me, too, because I'm a kid who started rapping when he was seven years old, with lots of views on YouTube, who performs in concerts and gets to meet lots of folks. But when you really start to think about it, every single one of us is totally unique. God made us that way.

We're all one of a kind.

I've been blessed to do some amazing things over the last five years, and I'm excited about the chance to spend some time with you and share those special moments. How I started to sing and rap and begin my musical journey. The things I've heard and seen and the places I've been. Some of the funny and crazy experiences I've had and the stories behind some of the songs and videos. Also to talk about my family and friends, and the important things that matter the most.

This book is also about you, because without the fans, none of this could have ever happened.

Most of all, I hope it's a chance to inspire you to know and believe that you are absolutely one of a kind and priceless.

Part One

SEVEN YEARS OLD, BUT MY FLOW IS SO COLD

Beginnings

It starts with a dream.

y story begins with a guy singing and a girl overhearing him. It's not me, though. I'm not in the picture yet.

This guy's at work, at one of those jobs nobody daydreams about, mopping floors. But that doesn't stop him from singing. Sometimes that's the only thing you *can* do in a depressing situation.

The girl says, "You need to be singing. You need to go do something with that, like try out for a talent show."

So this guy decides to give it a try. He has nothing to lose.

He's already lost everything, and I mean everything.

Leap of Faith

If you want to go farther, **dream big and work hard** **so you** can play harder.

The Georgia Dome is packed with ten thousand amateur singers, all hoping to be the next winner of *American Idol.* My cousin Mars is one of them.

His full name is Charles Marshall Manning, but he's always gone by Marshall. When he first began making music, his friends told him they'd never met anybody like him. "It's like you're from Mars," they told him. Mars was a natural nickname for Marshall, so it stuck.

It's January 13, 2010. Mars has been waiting for hours to go sing for thirty seconds in front of a judge at a table. There are six rows of judges on the field at the Georgia Dome, and groups of four have to go in front of them and perform. It's tough to sound good when you just start singing on the spot.

It's even tougher to go somewhere with ten thousand others and wait to probably get voted off. This is when you have to believe in yourself.

None of my family even knows Mars is trying out. He hasn't told anybody.

Things have been tough on Mars, though none of my family realizes how much. We do know that his mother, my father's sister, passed away recently.

Mars is definitely not in a good place in his life. He's working as a janitor for a restaurant, and it's there that a waitress setting up tables tells him he's got a great voice and should try out for *American Idol.*

That's exactly what Mars does.

He has hope. He also has faith. Those are the things you need to have in order to give it a shot.

My cousin borrows a friend's car and drives to downtown Atlanta, where the auditions will be. Then, after all the waiting and sitting around, Mars sings and actually makes it through!

It's the start of something really cool, but not in the way anyone expected.

My immediate family is not in the picture yet.

But very soon.

About Me

Know this, gotta be yourself for the world to notice.

I wasn't yet MattyB when I was born on January 6, 2003. I was named Matthew David Morris, and I have always been called Matt. My family, especially my dad, loves to come up with nicknames. MattyB was a childhood nickname because B (*bee*) rhymes with the *ee* sound in Matty and it just stuck. A lot of people ask me what the B stands for. I like to say it means "Be who you want to be." Because that is what I believe in.

I'm really an ordinary kid. I mean, I feel normal. I'm in sixth grade and love playing football. I go to school and then have football practice and then come home and work on homework. And sometimes record a song. I guess the music is the not-so-normal part of my life, though it sure feels normal to me.

I'll get to the music in a bit. But first, let me tell you about my family.

My father is Charles Blakey Morris, or Blake Sr. How would I describe him? Let's see . . . Smart, cool, handsome, athletic. (That's what he told me to say, anyway.)

My mother is beautiful, sweet, and loving. (That's what I came up with myself.)

The biggest thing about my parents is how protective they are with me and my siblings. They want the best for all of us, and they surround us with love and wisdom. Even in my own crazy journey the last five years, Dad and Mom have always asked what's the best thing for me as a kid—not as a performer or a brand—

whenever making any sort of decision.

I think it's fitting that Dad has four sons. He loves sports. All of us are different, but we're all competitive, too. Since I'm the baby of the sons, I often get picked on.

It's completely unfair, because I never do anything to deserve it. I'm never bothering my brothers or whining or tattling on them. I've never snuck in their rooms while they weren't home or borrowed their stuff without telling them, and I have *definitely* never stolen their Xbox controller batteries.

Never.

Really!

If you're not believing me, you should try to be more fair.

Okay, okay, but seriously, it's natural for my older brothers to sometimes pick on me, but it's in a good-natured way. We're all very close.

Sarah Grace? It's impossible to describe her quickly, but one word that comes to mind is joy. Not just the joy that she carries inside of

her, but the joy she gives to me and so many others.

Sarah Grace makes me happy, and she makes me laugh.

I have to add Mars to the mix, since he's the older brother we sort of adopted. He and I are the most alike. Not just because we love music, but in the way we think. Sure, he's older than me, but he often tells me our personalities are similar.

Mars likes to say that I'm his little buddy, and we're in this thing together. The music thing. It's cool and crazy to see what's happened with it. Together, Mars and I keep exploring what it all looks like.

So this is our family. We have no pets. As busy as we are, Mom and Dad have decided that something like a dog would be a little too much at this point in our lives. All of us kids are usually going in different directions, so it's hard enough for my parents to keep track of everybody.

I still think it'd be cool to have a really big dog. Like a German shepherd or, better yet, a Saint Bernard. We used to have a dog in the neighborhood named Charlie who would come over to play with us. My brothers and I would be playing basketball and see Charlie lying on his front porch. To protect Charlie from wandering into the street, his owners had an invisible electric fence and a collar on him that would warn him if he got too close to the property line. It would actually shock him if he went off the property.

When Charlie saw us outside playing, his tail would start wagging and he would pace back and forth, getting up the courage to run past the invisible electric fence. Eventually, he couldn't take it any longer and started running through the line to come over and play. I don't think the collar was on many times, or maybe he just didn't care, since he never hesitated to break through and circle the block and then come back for playtime with us. We'd reward Charlie by playing with him and giving him a snack for his bravery, then send him home when we heard his owner calling.

We live in Gwinnett County, Georgia. It's just north of Atlanta and is one of the largest counties in Georgia, with lots of fun towns and neighborhoods to grow up in.

My favorite things to do in my hometown are play golf, fish in the ponds, go to Town Center Park (a place you've seen in a lot of my videos), and hang out with neighborhood friends. We spend a lot of time in our backyards playing basketball and football and lacrosse.

And making the occasional music video, too.

Love at First Sound

I didn't know dozens and dozens of rap songs before I started to sing them. Mars would be the one I'd watch and listen to, and eventually learn from. I'm still learning from him today.

There was one song that I can remember loving. I can still hear it in my head:

The beat kicks in. The drum machine.

Then the "yeah" followed by four low "bum-bum-bum-bum"s on the piano as the rapping starts. So natural, so cool, so smooth.

MattyBRaps.com

Next the chorus comes, followed by a soaring female voice.

The song is "Empire State of Mind" by Jay Z and Alicia Keys. It's the first hip-hop song I remember listening to. The clean version, not the explicit one, of course. I loved it!

There's a video of me singing this song when I was around six. Not online, just one that Mars recorded. I'm not exactly singing, more like mumbling the words. There are lots of words to that song—it's not the easiest to rap when you're six. But I was loving it and really feeling it.

That's when the love first began. That's when I said, "I want to do that!"

Let's Make Some Music

In the beginning it was Mars in the booth
And a microphone and a beat
That was to capture the truth
That was spilled out of the heart of a young man
in his youth

—"Welcome to Mars," by MarsRaps

I can't imagine life without my parents. It's impossible. But my cousin Mars can, because he lost his mom.

In October 2003, Melinda Manning, Mars's mom and my aunt, was diagnosed with cancer. She received treatment and the prognosis was good. Two years later, in 2005, Mars moved with his family from Texas to Atlanta, because his mother was going to be working with my father. The following year, during spring break, they received some terrible news: the cancer had come back.

Mars went to college in August of 2006, and while he was home for Christmas that year, his mother passed away. When he returned to classes, Mars tried to deal with his mother's death. One way he did this was to write songs. He loved hip-hop and rap, so naturally he began to rap about everything he was going through. The hurt and the pain. He tried to express his feelings with music.

After dropping out of college, Mars soon found himself alone and barely managing to survive. That's when the waitress told him he should go on *American Idol.* He had her encouragement, and he also had nothing to lose.

Around this time he connected with my father. My dad was going through some tough times, as well. He's in the automobile industry, and his business was really struggling. He'd made some real estate investments that didn't turn out the way he wanted. The twenty-year-old family auto business was tanking, and he was at a pretty low point in his career.

It's cool to see the great things God can do when we're at those low points.

After competing to be a finalist on *American Idol* and writing some songs, Mars went to lunch with my father to see if he had any advice. Mars knew Dad was a good businessman, so maybe he'd be able to give him some ideas and encouragement.

"I made it to Hollywood week on *Idol*," Mars told my father.

Making it to Hollywood week meant he was among the top singers considered to be on the show. Mars then explained how he'd been writing songs and how he really wanted to do something with his music.

"I'll give you one of the CDs I made," Mars said. "It's got my songs on it."

After listening to his music and hearing my cousin's story, Dad ended up asking Mars if he wanted to move in with our family. Dad saw some potential and wanted to work with him on the music. My father's an entrepreneur, someone who likes to build things and start businesses. This music stuff was a lot more creative than the automobile industry, so he said, "Why not?"

Also, my parents could see that Mars needed a family. Mars basically told my father in their first meeting that he wanted my father in his life. So Mars moved in with us, taking a room in the basement.

I was six when Mars moved in. He was twenty-one. We all thought that maybe he'd be with our family for a couple of weeks.

Two weeks eventually became four years. And my cousin became my fourth brother, as well as my musical mentor.

Paving the Way

If you **believe in something** hard enough
You will go far **reach for** the stars
and **I believe in you**

—"I Believe in You," by MarsRaps

If you want to do something well, you need to learn as much as you can about it. This is exactly what Mars and my father did.

Mars had written and recorded some songs, and he wanted to do something with them. Dad was the businessman and entrepreneur, so they made a set of plans and steps. My father likes to call himself an excavator. He'll ask people things and might even be asking the wrong person the right question. But he'll keep asking and finding the right questions to ask the right people. Digging, digging, and digging, until he finds the best thing to do next.

The first thing was to figure out the industry and the music business, so they hired an attorney to help them learn about things like intellectual property and publishing and writing.

They quickly learned lots of things, like the basics of copyrights. There are lots of copyrights for music and they involve everything from the writing of the song to the actual recording of the music—the melody and lyrics. Writing and recording a song isn't always so simple these days, especially when there are lots of people involved in the process.

Dad and Mars learned how songs could be valuable for a long time and how they generated money in the form of royalties. When you hear that word, just think of the sound *cha-ching*.

They learned about the various roles that we would soon all find ourselves in: the "artist" and the "producer," the "songwriter" and the "label." How would all of these people work together to make the songs and then get the songs out to listeners?

Mars needed an online presence, and everything told them that YouTube was important. By 2008, they had watched Facebook get

bigger than Myspace, so by 2010, they figured that You-Tube was the place they needed to be.

Dad and Mars knew they needed content to put on YouTube—videos to go along with the songs. So Mars researched what kind of camera to get and how to edit videos and the right sort of equipment required for shooting.

On January 22, 2010, MarsRaps was the name my cousin gave himself. The first video he uploaded is called "Pants Up," and it's hilarious. It's got an Eminem-sounding melody and funny lyrics. The video was introduced with this message:

Marshall "Mars" Manning is a Hollywood-bound rapper and singer who was shown with his "Golden Ticket" during the January 13, 2010, "Atlanta Auditions" episode of *American Idol.*

Mars was there when "General" Larry Platt performed his notorious "Pants on the Ground" sensational hit and was inspired by the general to heed his wise words, thus quickly writing and recording a parody version entitled "Pants Up."

Mars was once a victim of SPS, "Sagging Pants Syndrome," but since the general's impartation, Mars has decided to "hike up" his attitude on the subject.

American Idol had shown the "Pants on the Ground" video during the Atlanta auditions, and the song became a craze for a while. So Mars did his parody of the whole idea. He celebrates belts and suspenders:

Y'all act like you've never seen a belt or suspenders before,
just a plain white tee and capri.
No, Mars, those are shorts.

Little known fact: the guy in the black cap and shades wearing a shiny belt buckle and Beats headphones around his neck happens to be my father.

A week later, Mars and my father uploaded "Romeo," an original song by Mars. This one was more of a serious love song. With each song released, they were learning things. What to do. What *not* to do. Some things they got right, while others they didn't. They were learning and making mistakes and figuring things out.

Dad and Mars say that while doing all this, spending time and money on the music Mars was making, God was planning and preparing for something else. They'd been working together a year and a half before something came along and surprised everybody.

That something was me.

How You Learn

Knowledge is power, so I am learning by the hour.

Learning isn't just something you do in a classroom listening to a teacher. You can learn at any moment of any day. Here are some lessons I've gotten from my parents and Mars and, yes, even my siblings:

1. **Be curious.** We should keep our curiosity, and not just for the things we love. Have a sense of wonder and interest in everything: a place you've never been before; a weird type of food; a hobby you'd never do; a person who seems odd. There's always more to discover, and the only way you're going to find it is by staying curious.

2. **Listen.** So many of us, including me, don't listen very well. We're so used to being able to share our opinions online somewhere that we don't usually wait to hear what others have to say. Let people explain things to you and ask them questions. Try to find out why things happened and how things are built and what causes one thing to lead to another.

3. **Don't be afraid to look stupid.** Sometimes asking questions makes us appear foolish, and sometimes stepping up and doing things makes us look completely dumb. But how

will you ever know if you can do something if you're unwilling to try it out?

4. Read. There's just no better way to fill your head with knowledge and stories.

5. Participate. Do things with others—your family or friends or church or schoolmates. Get out in your neighborhood. Build and create and discover and just do something. Experiences allow us to learn.

This is my top-five list, but there is one more thing that I would say trumps all of these and that is to GIVE. When we are first starting out, we want to be successful. We want to succeed, and we want things to go our way all the time. But that is not life. If you work hard and believe in yourself, there is no limit to what you can achieve. When you reach the goal, it feels great. However, what you give back is what counts the most. The only thing better than reaching your goals and accomplishing your dreams is the giving that you do along the way.

I'm not saying I do all these things perfectly all the time. Sometimes when my parents talk to me I don't hear a thing they've said. Sometimes Mars spends all this time explaining something about the business and I sort of zone out on him. I should read more and ask more questions.

One thing I am great at, however, is being willing to look like a fool in order to learn something.

That is how I ended up making the first song I ever released online.

Let's See What Happens

It's not **all about you,**

I think **I can rap,** too!

I remember the moment well.

It was a Saturday, and my best friend, Carson, and I went downstairs, where we found Mars playing Xbox.

"Will you listen to my song?" I asked him.

Ever since Mars moved in with us, I'd been going down to the basement to see him and hang out. Sometimes I would go into his room and show off some new dance moves. I'd listen to all his songs, and not only did I try to sing along with them, I wanted to perform them.

"Hey, Mars. Can I dance for you?"

So Mars would put on one of his songs and I'd bust out my little-kid moves. Mars would just be sitting there laughing. Sometimes he looked genuinely surprised.

"Let me see you do that again," Mars would say.

So on this day, I wanted to show him one of my songs. It wasn't the first time I'd done this. I'd written a few of them and had occasionally shown him the lyrics or even rapped a little for him. Mars nodded and paused his game to watch us. Carson started hitting a book to make a beat while I began to rap. I had my cousin's attention, and he even started moving his head to the beat.

I'd mixed together Taio Cruz and Justin Bieber and a few other songs to make my own original song. Mars recorded me on his iPhone while I rapped.

"Matt, that was really good," Mars said when I finished.

"I want to do it," I told him. "I want to make a video and put it online."

I was totally serious. I'd never been more serious in my long life of seven years.

Mars and my father weren't the only two people who'd been learning lots in the last eighteen months. I had been learning, too: seeing how Mars wrote lyrics and made the music on his computer. Listening to how he rapped. Noticing how he would weave together his own words to make a cool song. Studying the way he made a video and then edited it together.

"I want to put something up on YouTube," I said.

Mars just smiled. Eventually, he'd call my father and ask him what he thought.

"He really wants to do this," he told Dad.

My dad loves ideas and has a big imagination. He also likes to try things out. In this case, Dad liked the idea. Both of them thought that maybe this would be a great way to promote Mars's songs and videos.

"Okay, go for it," Dad told us. "But if you're going to do it, do it right. Get the 7D camera."

That meant plotting out the video and editing it and making sure it sounded as good as possible.

"Let's see what happens," Dad said.

So Mars recorded me with his Canon 7D SLR camera as I was

rapping lyrics over a kid-friendly parody of "Eenie Meenie" by Sean Kingston and Justin Bieber.

I was seven and happened to be missing my two front teeth. I just rapped with some of the lyrics Mars and I wrote together. The video consisted of me rapping into the microphone with my headphones on.

The music started, and I announced my arrival to the world.

Then I began to talk and set the stage:

Before that, I had been just ordinary Matt with a cool older cousin named Mars who rapped.

But suddenly, I was the one rapping.

There ain't never been another me.
No other Matty B
None at my age with the flow this cold, see.

That's how it started. No long meetings in big conference rooms with music industry executives. Nope, just a kid who wanted to rap like his big cousin. Mars filmed it and edited it in Final Cut Pro 7, just like with his own videos. Then we put it online to see what would happen.

I went to bed as Matt Morris. When I woke up, I was MattyB.

Seven Ways to Make a Video Go Viral

Turn your passion into action.

1. Pick a popular song that everyone loves.

2. Be yourself while you sing and perform it.

3. Do a good job with everything—the sound, the filming, the editing.

4. Take it seriously but not *too* seriously.

5. Bring a TON of passion and personality!

6. Don't be shy or hold back.

7. Oh, and yeah—it helps to have both your front baby teeth missing, to put the whole thing over the top.

The View from Here

A **dream** becomes **reality.**

The next morning, my father knocked on the door to Mars's room. It was 6 A.M., but Dad had some important news he couldn't wait to share.

"Mars—the video already has close to a half a million views," he said.

I was still sleeping, but I would learn this news later.

My cousin got out of bed and probably wondered if he was dreaming. You see, they'd been working hard to try to get views for Mars's videos. That's something I heard Dad and Mars talk about a lot. How to get more attention, more eyeballs on our page.

Five hundred thousand views in twenty-four hours?

There was no way. Mars had to pinch himself. But sure enough, the number was real.

It was unbelievable.

Right after I got up and went into the family room, they told me.

"That's cool," I said. Mars and my father could only laugh and tease me. I didn't understand the numbers and what they meant. What they *really* meant. I thought they were good and that it was cool, but not as cool as a new pair of Nikes.

"Just ignore the comments," Mars told me. "It is normal for people to not believe in your dream. You have done something amazing, but they will still find reasons to criticize you. Just shake off the haters."

The more views, the more haters. That was what they told me.

All I knew was I had a fun time singing and recording.

"Can we do more?" I asked.

It turns out they'd already been talking about the next one. I could just feel something different in the air. I could tell by the way they spoke that something was up.

You know what I mean. Like the times your parents might suddenly seem worried and talk in hushed tones, as if you have no idea what's going on. Or when an older brother keeping a secret might do a bad acting job. Or when something great has happened and you can just feel something changing.

Something great *was* happening. The numbers just kept going up. The last time I looked—wait, hold on a sec . . .

Okay, so yeah, it's up to 5,453,578 views as of this writing.

But back to June 2010. We began thinking and dreaming and praying.

What could we do next?

Hello, World

Maybe we can change the world.

If you have just one minute to sum up who you are, what are you going to say?

For the second video we made, we tried to do just that. Introduce who MattyB was. It didn't have to take long.

Mars knew me well enough to know what I enjoyed. I've always loved to make things, like drawing different sorts of creatures and animals and coloring them and then cutting them out. Even though I was only seven years old, I had a desire to create.

So music and performing just seemed like a natural fit. It made sense. It also made sense to share some of my creations on the camera, while putting my hopes and dreams out there.

The message in the second video we put up said it all.

Dreams are not something you can only have if you're a grown-up. My actual dream was to be a rapper *and* an artist. I wanted to be what the world had not seen before and share my message so it could spread further.

It was my desire to inspire others with my music, even if I was just a kid.

And so it began.

Chyeah

I'm literally lyrical at seven—
strange for **my age.**

You might have heard me use the word "chyeah" in my early songs when I was first starting to rap and post my videos, so I just wanted to say something about what this word means.

Sometimes, you need something to get you warmed up. Like before you play a football game, you stretch out. If you're going to start busting out a rhyme to a funky beat, then it helps to have one single word that puts you in the right frame of mind.

Chyeah.

Maybe you're about to say something amazing, and you don't have backup singers or cheerleaders to cheer you on. So you cheer yourself on.

Chyeah.

Occasionally, you need more than just a "right!" or a "yes!" or a "sure, sounds great!"

Chyeah.

Perhaps you need to wrap things up, to stop the song and say good-bye in a less formal sort of way. To say, "Yeah, I'm done for now, but you better keep your eyes out, 'cause MattyB's gonna be back and better than ever before, and hold on, 'cause it's gonna be soon." But you don't have time to say *all* that.

So you just go:

Chyeah.

Feel Free to Be a Goof

At seven years old,
I had them all perturbed.

Mars had done a parody version of a popular song and made a music video for it. In it, Mars is describing his first love, so he starts by saying, "Young love! Guard your hearts now."

When I started recording my version of the same song, I did the same thing when the song began.

"Young love," I said. "Guard your hearts now."

Mars stopped the music but kept recording our conversation.

"Matt—what are you doing?"

I laughed. "I just wanted to say that," I said.

So we kept going and as it turned out, Mars left this quote in there along with my explanation for why I did it.

Sometimes acting goofy just works, so you have to go with it!

ONE WORD
I LOVE TO SAY:

Debatable

Start Dreaming Today

Who says it matters what your age is?

We all need someone who believes in us: parents, brothers, sisters, cousins.

I thank God that I have all of those.

But more than that, I need to thank God that he believes in me and wants the best for me. As long as I trust him and give things over to him, good things can happen.

Things take time. Growing up and figuring things out, then growing a little more.

Seven seems so young, but a seven-year-old can still dream.

Ten seems like you're getting there, but eighteen sure seems so far away.

Twelve seems on the verge of something big, but I still have lots to learn.

So try to wake up with a sense of wonder each day.

What can I do today?

What dreams do I have?

What do I want to say and do?

Who am I, and how can I share that with others?

I don't think you have to know yourself completely all at once. I think each day allows us to know a little something more about who we are.

Both the simple things and the really hard ones, we can deal with all of them each day. We just have to believe in ourselves and find others who do the same. And look up to Heaven, knowing we're loved.

Someone is always watching over us. He wants the best for us, too. So why not dream big, since he'll always be bigger than our imaginations?

That's 'cause he created them, just like he created us.

Secret Seven

Some things I can't share,
'cause my spy tools are rare.

There's something I've never told anybody. Well, I told the whole world, but nobody believed me. Mars and I know the truth, though.

I used to be a secret agent.

I was one when I was seven.

The whole seven-year-old rapping thing? It was just a cover-up. My day job. Same with school and family and all that. Cover-ups.

Forget James Bond.

The name's B. MattyB.

Dad, Mars, and I once went down to Florida for my brother's baseball tournament. Dad instructed Mars and me to hit the beach and "knock out" a quick music video. We agreed, as long as we could ride bikes to the local city of Seaside afterward to get some ice cream.

On our way home, Mars told me that keeping

my imagination alive was one of the most important things I could ever do. Then he revealed his big secret: Mars used to be a secret agent.

As we rode back to the house on our tandem bike, Mars showed me his secret hideout and told me stories of fighting bad guys. It was like anything he could come up with, he had done it. Not only done it, but he was the best at it. I decided to share my big secret with Mars, too. At seven years old, I was also a secret crime-fighting agent. We were rappers by day and crime fighters when no one was watching.

Sometimes I'd have to break out some kind of vicious karate chop on the bad guys or maybe just scare them with my lightsaber. Mars could stun them with an 808 beat and a blast of Auto-Tune.

After the bad guys would be hauled away, we could head down to the Dairy Queen where I'd get an Oreo Blizzard and share it with Mars.

I like my Blizzards shaken, not stirred.

Appropriately Awesome

Dreaming 'bout the future from my swing set, and I am wondering if I could be the king next.

For about six months, Mars would release a video for his stuff, while at the same time releasing one of mine. But while visiting and performing at a church in Indiana for his latest album, Mars realized something.

This whole MattyB thing that we'd done for fun was totally blowing up.

Dad and Mars were on the road when they learned that the website Yahoo! had put me on their front page with my parody rendition of "California Girls." It was the seventh video of mine we'd released. Suddenly, it had over a million hits.

Mars likes to say that I made it look so easy—that I had charisma and was cute. Now, if you look at those dance moves in "California Girls," I think I sure had a long way to go. And as far as being "cute"? Well . . .

"I have to clear the air about something," I said in the video. "I had to get a haircut, because people kept saying I was cute and looked like Justin Bieber."

Big, long sigh.

"There is *nothing* cute about rappin'. *Capiche?*"

Okay, so maybe a *little* cute. But we heard lots of parents tell us

that they liked my music because it was clean and fun and the lyrics were responsible and appropriate. My father said that as long as there's no profanity or dirty stuff or drugs or violence in the cover songs, then it was fair game.

"We can have swag and laughs and do comedy and make it fun and be edgy," Dad said.

The music that Mars had been making had started out being written from a really dark place in his life. Then he began making music that in some ways went to the opposite side of that, with his parodies. Now he was helping me make something in the middle. Raps from a seven-year-old perspective that are fun-loving and cool without being dark or too serious.

The King of Pop

y two favorite songs by Michael Jackson are "Thriller" and "Man in the Mirror." But he's got like two hundred other great songs.

When people talk about the greats—like the *greats* of the greats—Jackson is among them, along with Elvis and The Beatles and Madonna and Garth Brooks and Stevie Wonder and Whitney Houston.

If you've never checked out Michael Jackson, you have to. When he first began making hits, people couldn't just type "Michael Jackson" into Google. They would hear him on the radio and see him on television, and they'd have to leave the house and go buy his album at the record store. On vinyl records, which could get scratched. Or cassettes that took forever to rewind. Or even something called eight-tracks (which I still don't quite understand).

A song like "Don't Stop 'Til You Get Enough" makes you want to start bobbing your head. Then there's his really big hit called "Billie Jean." This one is all about the beat.

Boom-tick boom-tat boom-tick boom-tat. Buh dum bum buh bum dum dum doom.

Supposedly the song was mixed almost one hundred times to

get it sounding just right. The drum beat sounds simple, but also absolutely original. They can only belong to the song "Billie Jean." (I'd get to do my version in 2011.)

There's the classic hit "Beat It" with the dance music mixed with the hard rock guitar. "Wanna Be Startin' Something" with all its *ch-ch-ch*'s with drums and beats and more *ch-ch-ch*'s.

But "Thriller"? There's only one "Thriller." It's the best.

The video is awesome. There are probably hundreds of videos online showing groups doing the dance. I bet you've maybe even tried it yourself, right?

My other favorite, "Man in the Mirror," was on the *Bad* album.

This song is inspirational and one that really sums up what I'm trying to do with my music. Not just get people dancing and smiling and feeling good, but also believing in themselves.

Michael Jackson started making music at an early age. His music has inspired millions, including me. I still believe that I can do some pretty amazing things. I'm continuing to try. I hope you are, too.

My School

Train up a child in the way he should go.

Proverbs 22:6

Wesleyan School is awesome.

It's a Christian K-12 school located twenty miles north of Atlanta. Approximately a thousand students attend it. The teachers and all the programs (especially sports) are excellent. The school feels more like a college campus, or so I've heard people say. I haven't known anything other than Wesleyan, so I can't compare. These aren't the reasons my school is awesome, though.

It's because their whole goal with everything is about honoring and glorifying Jesus Christ. That's why they started, and that's what they strive to do every day. Anything that happens at Wesleyan—whether it's a football game or a science project or the artist market or a missions trip—is done in a place that's focused around Christ, which is very important to me and my family.

The classes tend to be smaller, at least in middle school, with maybe twenty students in them, and most classes only have one teacher per class. The teachers are awesome and really care about helping us learn and grow.

Faith is first, and the students are second. We're encouraged to dream big at Wesleyan. It's the perfect place for me to be.

If I Was Old Enough

You never know what **tomorrow** will bring,
because **timing** is everything.

My father was in an airport when a song came on that made him stop and listen. In the past, he probably would have completely ignored it. He wouldn't be paying attention. But these days, Dad pays attention to all sorts of songs.

He immediately called Mars.

"I just heard this song. We gotta do a cover of this song."

"What's the song?" Mars asked.

" 'Boyfriend' by Justin Bieber."

Mars knew the song, of course.

"He's singing to a girl," Mars said.

It wasn't exactly the perfect song for a kid.

"Well—it will be outrageous for Matt and have a ton of humor."

So that's exactly what happened. When Dad was back home, we talked about the song in the kitchen. We were playing it and got the vocal range right for me.

It didn't take weeks or even days. It was done right there, on the spot.

It took about two hours to record the song. We went to Town Center Park and made a quick video for it. Then we posted it, and a couple of days later, we actually saw it playing in the Mall of

Georgia at the food court, which meant it was likely playing in many other malls across the country. Our video was placed on a playlist on Justin Bieber's YouTube channel, and it quickly grew in views. After just six hours' worth of work.

The video had millions of views in a very short amount of time, and we saw our social networks start to take off.

Simple, right?

Well, yeah, sure. But there were other things involved. Three and a half years have given us a little perspective.

How could we explain everything that had happened so suddenly? Putting a fun little video up that went viral . . . well, that was rare, but it does happen. Half a million views? That was wild, but then it happened again. And again. And again.

And then *this* happened.

"It's all about timing," I've heard lots of people say. Even my parents and Mars have said that. But timing always puts stuff in the "coincidence" category. My family and I believe it comes from God in the "favor" category.

We do know that at the time, there weren't as many people doing what we were doing: a young kid covering popular songs or making parodies of hit songs on YouTube. Rapping lyrics from a kid's point of view. Having fun and making funny content for other kids.

Nowadays, you'll find lots of acts doing this. *Lots.* But at the time, YouTube was new and exploding, and I was able to find my place. My "niche," as Mars and Dad will say. So yeah—in that way, timing played a key part.

But it was also a perfect choice of a song for me to sing. It's like in a singing competition, the judges always say it's about the song choice. And Dad was right, it was the perfect song to do our take on.

The falsetto was a first for me at that age. I was just growing and evolving. Just like right now, as I turn thirteen and become an official teen, my voice is starting to change. None of us are freaking out or even worried. I'm going to sound like I sound as I get older.

We didn't have a plan about how I sounded at seven, and we don't have a plan now. We'll just keep doing what we're doing and growing and changing and figuring things out. Mars and Dad have taught and encouraged me that I'll always be able to perform. Emotion and personality and expression are the keys.

Some of the greats—the truly great ones—don't have the most

flawless and perfect voices or performances. They *do* have the most emotion and personality. The most passion, heart, and soul put into their music.

I was learning to sing better and perform better, things like the right timing and the right song choice and some new reaching in my vocal performance.

All those things helped.

But Mom and Dad and Mars and all of us realize that more than any and all those things listed above, it was God who orchestrated the whole thing.

God can make anything happen. It can take many years or it can happen instantly.

The key is to allow it to happen and to have faith that it will.

And then—this is even more important . . .

To never forget who allowed the good things to happen in the first place.

Broken Wings

I believe that you're **a star!**
I just wanna see you be the person that you are!
—"I Believe in You" by MarsRaps

My cousin Mars first heard the hip-hop artist 2Pac while riding a bus on the way to football practice. The song was "Changes," and that's exactly what the song did to him. It changed him. Things weren't going to be the same. He'd be a hip-hop fan and suddenly start dreaming of making songs as powerful as that one.

By the time Mars was twenty, he found himself making some really bad decisions. He'd never blame those mistakes on anyone other than himself, but he does acknowledge the influence that

the music he listened to and the artists he looked up to had on his young life.

Mars realized how big an impact music can make on a person. That's why he wanted to set a good example and a high standard for the music he would make. He decided to make his music based around wholesome and positive things. He would write his own songs or cover other people's songs, but he'd make it his own with a positive message.

This technique was exactly what Mars would later do with me.

"Let's make it our own," he would always say.

Sure, I was only seven, but it didn't mean that I couldn't share my experiences with satire or comedy from a kid's perspective.

We all have something we can share.

Mars once said, "I believe we only live in this body once, and the choices we make today will impact the outcome of our future, as well as that of those around us. I encourage you to take life seriously and make the best choices you know how to make with what you have."

I'm taking life seriously, along with having some fun with the musical choices we've been making. Being a positive role model and being responsible with your music does *not* mean you can't have fun.

Chyeah!

TWO MOMENTS THAT
HAVE MADE ME HAPPY:

First billion views
and
when my team won
our sixth-grade football
championship

The Jedi Rap Master

**Purple shades, Legos, and Kooky pens, too,
you never know the crazy stuff
that I'mma get into.**

So it was summer 2010. We were on a roll, putting out a video every two weeks. Not just one by me, but also one by Mars. And the rhymes kept flowing.

Usually, the process was fast and simple. We'd get together, Mars would lay down a beat, and then we'd start to throw out lyrics.

For instance, at the time I had this cool pair of purple sunglasses. So Mars threw out some line talking about my purple shades and shopping with my penny jar at the mall.

The songs weren't trying to have me sound like a twenty-five-year-old. They were about me being me.

Star Wars, Legos, and my skateboard, these were the types of things that made sure I was never bored.

Mars said that there are a few things on YouTube: entertainment, talent, music. But something else that's important is comedy—being funny.

With each video, we'd try to focus on good music, lyrics from my life, and being fun and funny. We also had a message, which was always about following your dreams and believing in yourself.

I'd share my experiences in the lyrics, and Mars would remember back to when he was seven, eight, or whatever age I might be at the time. My cousin can definitely relate, too. He was making up raps at those very same ages. He still remembers one of the early poems/songs he wrote. Here's an excerpt:

Life is full of ups and downs
Lots of smiles but then come frowns
Such good times enjoyed by few
But bad times come when skies aren't blue.

Mars says he was always a sensitive kid and would secretly write poems and record songs, raps, and poems on his boom box. He never really knew what to do with all these things. Then as he got older, he became more familiar with hip-hop and rap. After his mother passed away and he dropped out of college, he began writing a lot more. He'd write a song every other day and ended up with over a hundred songs.

Ten of them were made into the recording Mars gave to my father. Those ten songs suddenly changed our lives.

By the time Mars would move in with us and begin releasing his own music with my father, he had between 150 and 200 songs he'd not only written but had recorded in one form or another.

Those songs—and all the songs that we've both written since—are memories and pieces of ourselves, experiences put to melodies. They can be stories or even just feelings. So Mars and I always talked about things like that.

"Okay—so this is going to be about your first crush," Mars said. "How do you act? How do you treat the girl?"

We'd try to find ways to express those experiences.

Since I had lost my two front teeth, some of the words I would rap came out sounding funny. Sometimes that's what we wanted, to make it sound silly. But other times, I couldn't get the lyrics right. It would drive me crazy and make me want to give up.

"I can't do it!" I'd say.

Suddenly, Mars was no longer my cousin but my coach. He'd look straight at me.

"Yes you can," Mars said. "You can do anything you put your mind to, if you believe in yourself. Just trust me. One day, you're going to be great. If you keep doing this and you trust me, one day you're going to be traveling on an airplane to California and New York!"

I stuck with it. Partly because Mars encouraged me and partly because I'm so competitive—but mostly because it's just so much fun.

The Not-So-Grand Plan

Many are called, but few are chosen.

Matthew 22:14

With each new song and every new video of mine we'd put up, we would learn something new. There was never any sort of grand decision for Mars to focus solely on helping me with my music. He was just seeing how suddenly the things we were doing were having success.

"Sticking and getting traction," he'd say.

But Mars saw something else then, too. He saw my father being able to do something special with one of his sons—the same sort of stuff he'd been doing with Mars.

"You have this ability to connect with people," Mars said. "And I'm able to help write and create content."

That combination, along with my father's business experience, had started to work. Thankfully, it has been working to this day.

The timing was also important. People like Justin Bieber, Cody Simpson, One Direction, and Austin Mahone began popping up and becoming stars. YouTube was the thing that really helped launch many of them. So there were these young singers out there that we could watch and observe what they did.

"We can do something like that, but we can control our own destiny," Mars and Dad would say. "We can control our content."

So we kept making music and uploading videos, always watching to see what fans liked and didn't like, hoping to continue reaching our goals.

Reality Check

Focus and keep a level head.

After those first videos went crazy with hundreds of thousands of views, this was how much I changed as a person:

Love

From the start, she stole my heart.

L et me tell you about the most beautiful girl in the world.

She laughs a lot. Sometimes she teases by acting as if she doesn't like me. But she never hesitates to say she's my biggest fan.

Sometimes we sit in the park or on the couch and she tells me stories. These are some of the best moments of my life.

If I try to rap for her, she'll always take over and come up with her own lyrics.

Maybe one day I'll meet someone else as special as this girl.

But she'll still never be Sarah Grace, my sister.

I'm her favorite brother. Well, at least I'm one of four favorite brothers. It just depends on her mood. But she's *my* favorite and always will be.

Just the Way You Are

**Got no time for the haters.
I love her just the way God made her.**

Here's the story behind the first video that Sarah Grace made with me.

"I want to dedicate this song to my little sister, Sarah Grace. She's only four, and she was born with special needs. I think she's the prettiest girl in the whole world, and I'm pretty sure you'll agree, too."

That's how I started my cover of the Bruno Mars song "Just the Way You Are."

We'd been making songs and releasing them online and having fun, but something was different with this one. Not just because of the number of views. That has nothing to do with it. It was all the comments and the responses we were seeing.

There's just something about Sarah Grace. People love her.

The idea came after my mother had new pictures taken of Sarah Grace. She had this new dress on and looked adorable.

We'd been talking about me doing a cover of "Just the Way You Are." We all agreed that the subject could be none other than Sarah Grace. Sarah was special and beautiful in spite of being born with Down syndrome.

I loved introducing my little sister to the world. To show how I

love her for who she is. We've always been really close, so it was just natural to do a video about the bond between a brother and sister.

Hopefully, this encouraged people to accept and love others un-conditionally. To remind people to tell each other how much they are cherished.

Down the road, we would have other opportunities to share more about Sarah Grace.

Actually, we didn't even have a choice. She'd had her debut and was going to be filmed one way or another!

She would make very sure of that.

All in the Family

**If you are wondering about me,
it started in my family tree.**

I think this performing and rapping thing isn't such a surprise for our family. Mars was already doing it, so he could definitely relate. But who I am also has a lot to do with my mom and dad and my brothers and sister.

My father says that his mom was always into poetry and drama, and of course these are two things that I do every day. Dad's an entrepreneur, so he's continually showing his creative side with insights related to the business. Mom has always been very artistic and creative, and it comes out in lots of different ways. She's always helping with costumes and designing the sets. She's really good with styling, whether it's our home or the set of a video.

I grew up watching my big brother Blake Jr. being involved in drama and art. He's an amazing drummer, too. John is the natural athlete, but he's not the stereotypical "jock." That's 'cause he's really smart. And then Josh is a very creative artist with drawing and painting, as well as taking after John with his skills in sports.

Then Sarah Grace . . . Well, you know what a natural she is.

I just happen to be formed in a certain way, so that I enjoy being up in front of people and performing. I like being the first to volunteer and go headfirst into whatever.

Being the one most known for my creativity doesn't mean I'm the most creative one in our family. My creativity just shows itself in *louder* ways.

How to Be a Good Friend

If you put **your mind to it,**
you can do it.

1. Be nice.

2. Answer questions honestly.

3. Show interest.

4. Pass the remote.

5. Focus on faces, not some screen.

6. Do something unique together.

7. If your friend's kite gets caught up in a tree, try your best to climb it.

8. Share in person, not just online or on the phone.

9. Try to stay friends even when they seem completely annoying (just maybe it could be about *you*).

10. It's fine if you like MattyB and your friend doesn't. We all have different tastes.*

---

* You can get them to change their minds. I have faith in you!

The Big Apple

Go MattyB!

Talk-show host Wendy Williams stood in front of the audience and cameras and welcomed me on the show.

"My next guest is a seven-year-old rapper and an Internet sensation. In the last few months, he's posted eighteen homemade videos on YouTube and he's received over eighteen million hits."

Chyeah!

"He's a first-grader from Atlanta, Georgia, and he's definitely on his way to superstardom. Please welcome the adorable rapper MattyB!"

I stepped onto the stage and looked out at a room full of women. There wasn't one guy in the whole room except for me, Dad, and Mars.

Before the show, I got to have my own green room with my name on it. If you don't know what a green room is, it's not a room that's literally green. It's the name for a special room for you to hang out and relax before you go onstage.

The song I'd perform was "Go MattyB." When I got to the part where I danced, everybody seemed to love it.

"You are as cute as you wanna be," Ms. Williams told me after my song.

She gave me some bling: sparkling shades, a matching rhinestone-studded nameplate on a chain, and a shiny grill.

Since *The Wendy Williams Show* was in New York City, I got a chance on that trip to visit the world's biggest toy store, FAO Schwarz. It was awesome, to say the least. It felt like ten toy stores in one. I had a hard time picking out a gift for Sarah Grace, but eventually I chose a Barbie. I met Chewbacca in the store, and I even got to play on the *Big* piano. Have you ever seen this? It's in the movie *Big* with Tom Hanks. And it really is big—you step back and forth on the giant keys, and they play notes just like a piano would.

We had something else in store while we were in New York. Something incredible.

I got a chance to meet with some record companies. I met a lot of nice people who complimented me on my songs and videos. That was really cool. That wasn't the "incredible" thing I was talking about, though, which was that we got to go to Dylan's Candy Bar. To say it's a candy shop is like calling the Super Bowl a football game.

Dylan's Candy Bar looks (and even smells) like it's *made* of candy. The wallpaper on the staircases have candy all over them. There are lollipop trees and songs about chocolate. It's like the real Willy Wonka chocolate factory. They say that there are over seven thousand different candies in Dylan's. Walking through the store was a little like stepping over a rainbow.

The most fun I had that day was selecting unique toys or candy for each of my brothers and for Sarah Grace. Even though it felt like a crazy field trip or vacation, the funny thing was that I was actually "working."

If this was what work looked like, I wouldn't mind doing a lot more of it!

Haters

Haters stay mad 'cause my feet stay crisp
and my hits stay big 'cause I do it like this.

The world is full of haters. Lots of them, just waiting to unleash something negative into the world.

It's so easy to do it nowadays, too. You can criticize on Twitter. You can make a mean comment on Facebook. You can write a whole blog about something or somebody you want to make fun of. You can even post a video on YouTube ripping something apart.

The bigger the person or thing, the more hate or negative comments they're going to receive—Taylor Swift or J. K. Rowling or Jimmy Fallon. It doesn't even have to be a person. It can be Chick-fil-A or Nike or the Dallas Cowboys or *Survivor*. People, shows, teams, and products. Consumers have come to see these as all the same thing: brands. But unlike Microsoft or Coca-Cola, people have feelings.

So I've learned something.

Never read the negative comments. Just stay away from them.

I figure there's enough hate in the world. Why waste my time? Why not skip over it and find something positive to focus on?

I love what I do. I love rapping about the good things in life, being upbeat and optimistic. That's what I'm going for.

There's an enemy wanting to bring me down, but there's a

bunch of fans out there who give me enough strength and love to be only positive.

The Bible tells us to think about good things, things that are noble and right and pure and lovely—admirable and excellent and praiseworthy sorts of things.

If you're gonna jump on some trending topic, then make sure it's about something positive and uplifting.

Taylor Swift is right when she says the haters are going to hate. So I move on and make music that's about fun, love, and positivity.

Get to Know Some YouTube

This is as good as it can get,

on the Internet.

Here are some things about YouTube.

After you reach a certain number of subscribers, you can request to be a partner channel. This is when you monetize, as my father puts it. It means you get paid for the videos you post.

Crazy, right?

Google runs ads on your video, then pays you as the content creator for a portion of the money they make from the advertisers.

The more views you get, the more money you make.

I didn't know you could get paid for these videos!

After my first check came, I decided to head back to Dylan's Candy Bar for a shopping spree. Oh wait—my parents said I have to save money. But I am allowed to pick out new Nikes, which is good enough for me!

Mars likes to say, "Content is king."

Dad likes to say, "Views are king."

Maybe I should just say, "I'm the king" and then make a video about it (oh wait, I did!).

Part Two

EVERYTHING'S GREAT, AND I JUST TURNED EIGHT

The Rock

No stopping me, I'mma B who I wanna B.

I n March 2011, we were invited to participate in a video that would be aired to a *much* different audience than the one I was used to.

This video would be watched by fans of WWE (World Wrestling Entertainment) and the professional wrestler and actor Dwayne Johnson, aka "The Rock."

This was around the time when The Rock was making a comeback in wrestling. The idea for the video was that The Rock would be talking to his archrival in WWE, John Cena. The Rock set it up by having a phone conversation in which he said he tried to talk to John Cena as a man, but instead he felt like he was talking to a child. So then they'd make it look as if Cena was going to show up in the video, finally talking to The Rock in person.

"Here's your final chance to talk like a man," The Rock said.

And that's when I'd enter looking all tough wearing one of Cena's jerseys. The Rock would then stand up and talk down at me. Literally talk down at me, since I only came up to his knees.

It was a fun bit to participate in, and it was amazing to be able to meet The Rock in person. The thing about this experience, however, was that it almost didn't even happen.

When WWE brought the opportunity to us, my father was hesitant. It was quite a different audience from those watching our videos, so Dad wanted to make sure it made sense. He just wasn't sure it was a natural fit.

After they gave us a script for the video, my father realized that it worked for their brand, sure, but it didn't work for ours. I was eight years old and had a lot of kids my age watching my videos. The last thing we wanted to do was to have me be in something we didn't think would be appropriate for our demographic.

My father went back and forth with WWE, all while the date to film the scene was approaching. Soon we would need to fly out to Los Angeles to film it, yet we weren't even sure if we were going to do it at all.

Finally we had to make a decision: do we head out to LA or do we stay put? So Mom, Mars, and I all ended up flying out west, even though we still weren't sure if it was even going to happen.

At one point, Dad called to say I wouldn't be in the video shoot. He was canceling the deal, because the script had not yet been finalized. Then it looked like it was on again. Then it wasn't.

Eventually, everybody decided that the right thing was to go to The Rock's house after all. I'd seen him in some movies I liked. I knew he'd appeared on Nickelodeon and Disney, in addition to being a superstar in wrestling.

They say some people seem larger than life. The Rock *is* larger than life, literally. When he greeted me, I felt like I was shaking hands with a giant. I don't know if I have ever met anyone that big.

At The Rock's house, there was a crew setting up, along with a bunch of other people. Everything was ready to go. The director was giving me instructions and getting prepared. There was just one problem.

Mars and Mom went over the final script, and they noticed some areas we still were not comfortable with. Even though it had been cleaned up, there were still some things that just were not right for us and our brand.

Our videos had all been about believing in yourself and following your dreams. This video was really different. After talking with my father on the phone, Mars ended up having to make a tough decision.

He had to say no.

I knew how big a deal this was. We'd flown all the way out there, and we were on the set, and all these people were expecting me to be in the video. How could we say no?

My parents and Mars stood firm, though. That's what you have to do when you believe in something. Even if it means having to go up to one of the biggest and strongest men on the planet and tell him no.

That's exactly what my cousin did.

The Rock is six feet five inches and weighs around 260 pounds, but it didn't matter. Mars went over to him to explain the situation.

"Excuse me, Mr. Johnson. I understand I'm in your home," Mars said. "We know this is your script, and this is your comeback. But we can't do this."

The cool thing was that The Rock was so incredibly gracious and kind. They talked things over and worked everything out. The Rock made the changes, and he was open to letting us do things the way we requested. As Mars said, it was about preserving our integrity and those things my parents had said we could not compromise. We never want to judge others, but we also want the right to say what is acceptable for us and to refuse to budge on that. We appreciated and respected The Rock's cooperation.

And I learned something pretty important that day.

You have to stand up for what you believe, no matter where you are and what the circumstance might be. Sometimes you might have to disappoint people. Sometimes you might have to change everybody's plans. Sometimes you have to stand up to something big. You might even have to stand up to Dwayne Johnson.

If so, you can always remember what it says in Psalm 78:35: "They remembered that God was their Rock."

The Video Blog

Time **to connect** on a whole **new level.**
It's **not just bass** and treble.

We decided to start MattyBVlogs in order to try to connect more with my fans. The videos had been so much fun, but they didn't always allow me to share different parts of my personality. I would receive a lot of questions and comments, so this would be my chance to share my thoughts online.

The first video went up on June 29, 2011.

We wanted to be able to show people what's behind the scenes of video shoots. A lot of questions came from that—who films you, and how do

you write your songs, and who is this Mars guy, and other things like that.

I'd be able to talk about video games I play and sports and other things I loved. I told everybody that Sarah Grace wasn't in my first vlog, but she definitely would be in future episodes, since she loved getting in front of the camera. Like, really, *really* loved being on camera.

I could share my home and my life and my computer and Legos and all that.

There'd never been some big plan or goal; we were just having fun figuring out how to entertain people.

Life is all about connecting, and there are so many ways you can do that.

Old School

Can I take it back one time in my rhyme?

I t's one thing to throw my raps over someone else's track, but it's another to do it *with* them in the booth. That's what happened with Vanilla Ice.

Here's a little background on Vanilla Ice, in case you don't know who he is. (And if you don't, please go online and check him out!)

The name he was born with is Robert Van Winkle. He grew up in Florida and Texas, and he became interested in dancing at a young age. He had some tough times during his childhood, because of hanging around the wrong people and doing the wrong things. Eventually he would become known for his dancing, because he hung out at clubs to get people's attention. After getting a manager, Vanilla Ice released his first album in 1989. On this album was a song called "Ice Ice Baby."

It would take a radio station in Georgia playing that song for Vanilla Ice to start getting some attention. He landed a deal with a record label, which put out his first record, called *To the Extreme*. "Ice Ice Baby" was on that album.

The album sold tons and went to the top of the charts. Suddenly, Vanilla Ice was known by everybody. He would end up going on tour with MC Hammer and even starring in some movies.

As we talked about a song to put a kid-friendly spin on, Dad suggested doing a classic. A lot of the songs that were suggested were unknown to me. You can't exactly think of a classic when you're eight, and you haven't heard tons of songs to begin with. But Dad and Mars talked about one that would be great, and then they played it for me.

This song rocked!

I didn't have to listen more than thirty seconds before I nodded and said, "Let's do it!"

I wanted to learn all the lyrics right away. The rapping was so natural, and the track stuck in my head for the rest of the day.

My dad had an idea, a pretty cool one. One of those *why not* sort of ideas.

Dad got a hold of the artist himself, reaching out and telling him about me and the things we were doing. He talked about the videos I had online and how much we loved his song and about the possibility of maybe doing something together.

Mr. Ice loved the idea. He was willing to get together and do something fun with "Ice Ice Baby." This was the first rap song in history to reach number one. Now I'd be performing it *with* the artist?

How awesome was that?

Vanilla Ice admitted that he wondered whether I had enough rhythm, since he knew I was eight. Could this kid really flow? That's what he was curious about before meeting me and observing my skills.

The first thing about working with Vanilla Ice was how much fun it turned out to be. Filming is usually fun, but this was a blast. This guy had done it big time. Watching his old videos and seeing him sing and dance—he was amazing. His dance moves resembled Michael Jackson's. The way he made it look so easy and so natural to just glide and turn. He could still do all those things, and he could still rap like nobody else.

Vanilla Ice was a really nice guy. That was cool to see, because he didn't have to come hang out and sing and dance with an eight-year-old. He not only did it, but he was really encouraging with me. He joked around a lot, and more than that, he actually seemed to be impressed with my raps and my moves.

I'd watch him and laugh. He'd rap and make a joke, and I'd just stare in amazement. This guy was who I wanted to be, maybe who I was starting to be. Shorter and younger but, yeah, still. We were brothers in a sort of way, just like Mars and me. Just like all rappers are.

Vanilla had so many phrases and sayings and raps that he was throwing out, even when there was no music playing. It was like he had a thousand lyrics that he could just keep producing, line after line. And I just kept smiling and laughing and thinking *this is so cool.*

Recording the song felt like being in class and having a teacher work with me individually. Except in this case, we both wore headphones, listened to a track, and performed. He would help me with my timing, with what I should and shouldn't be doing.

While shooting the video, we had a great time dancing and doing flips and wearing our white caps and singing "Ice Ice Baby" over and over again.

All along, Vanilla Ice kept saying nice things about me.

"This kid's got skills," he told all of us.

This meant a lot. I played it off with *oh yeah, I know I'm all that, so chyeah, I got this.* But come on! Vanilla Ice—the guy behind "Ice Ice Baby"—was giving me compliments and advice? So Mars was the first rapper/adopted brother who came into our family. And Vanilla Ice was the second.

Vanilla left us with some advice for anybody who wanted to go out and do what he did. He encouraged me to go after tomorrow and believe in my dream.

I was thankful to be doing just that, following my dreams. And I was even more grateful to have someone patting me on the back and telling me I could do this—and even helping and teaching me a few things. A few new moves and raps, all while having a good time doing it. I want to send him big-time thanks.

That's what I learned about Vanilla Ice. You could be great and talented, but you had to have fun. Maybe we'd work together in the future.

As Vanilla Ice would say, word to your mother.

Meeting Celebrities

I have **seen you** on my TV,
and now **you are right** in front of me.

All of a sudden, I was starting to meet celebrities. People I'd seen in videos and on television and singers I'd heard of—I was now suddenly talking to them. I've been so fortunate to meet sports stars and media figures and lots of people inspiring others. Here are some thoughts about what to do or not do when you meet someone famous.

1. **Act Normal.** Okay, so maybe you don't consider yourself "normal," but you know what I mean. Freaking out is not your normal self. Nor is suddenly becoming completely terrified. Act as if you're talking to your brother or a friend.

2. **Treat Them Like Normal People.** There's a phrase you might have heard: "He puts his pants on one leg at a time." This is to say that everybody really is the same. Of course, some people can dunk basketballs or can sing like angels. But they're still just *people*, so remember to treat them that way.

3. **Listen.** The worst thing someone can ever do is talk and talk and talk, without letting the other person have a chance to speak. That's in any relationship, by the way.

4. Talk. On the other hand, make sure you say something. I've had this happen a lot where a girl will meet me and be speechless. It's cute—it makes me smile. I understand, especially when they're young. But as for myself, I always want to be able to say *something* to the celebrity I'm meeting.

5. Ask Questions About Them. This is a chance for you to learn, but it's also a chance to have them share something about themselves. You never want to get too personal, but at the same time, people like to talk about things that have happened to them or that mean something to them. Like when someone asks me, "What's Sarah Grace up to?" or something like that.

6. Respect Their Time. If you do meet a celebrity, realize how many times people are stopping them to take pictures and say something. Be brief and understand that they have lives to live, too.

7. **Share the Love.** Anytime I've met someone in the public eye who spends some time with me, I tell the world about it. Tweet or share a photo on Instagram. "Katy Perry is even more awesome in person than her videos!" Or something like that.

8. **Compliment.** Once again, remember that people are people. Treat them like you'd want to be treated, and say something nice about them. Sometimes you might be so surprised to see them that you forget to tell them what a great player they are or how you love their movies. Everybody loves (and needs) to be reminded about what they do well. Even those famous folks!

THREE TOTALLY TERRIFIC THINGS

1. KD7 "What The" Sneakers

2. Lacrosse

3. Discovering waterslides when I was seven

Girls, Part Duh

There are some things I know without a doubt, but you're the type of girl I will never figure out.

Sometimes having all these raps online—all these lyrics recorded and shared for all to see—might make it seem like I'm always ready with words. Full of the right things to say.

Sometimes, though, I gotta admit . . . I'm speechless.

I don't fully understand girls. They're fascinating, but they're also quite *strange*. They tend to change day to day. The things they say, the way they act, the sort of looks they might give. One day, they're all *yay*, and then the next, they're all *yikes*. Guys don't change. My buddies act the same way yesterday and today and tomorrow. But girls . . .

Girls change like the weather. I could have all the words, but I can never know which ones I might need to use.

These girls—they really are something else. I wonder if I'll understand them more when I'm grown up.

Probably not.

Unlike a video game that's played till the end and once you're done, you're done, you're never done with girls. I know from being around Mom and Sarah Grace, and from all the other girls I've met. Every day—every *moment*—is a new experience.

I watch with wonder. Complete and speechless wonder.

One Great Tune

**Get a good idea and then use it,
that is all it takes to create good music.**

L et's talk about music for a moment. I've learned to start to
love a little bit of everything, 'cause I learn something from
everything:

> A pop singer with a beat you can dance to and a cool, new
> sound.
>
> A singer/songwriter sharing a story and playing just a guitar.
>
> The country singer who sings a sweet song in her own
> unique way.
>
> A Christian band jamming away with amazing joy and faith.
>
> A classic rock song that I've heard in commercials and finally
> hear the whole thing and get blown away.

Of course, hearing the latest hip-hop track and getting new inspiration.

Different songs all can share similar elements. A melody. Verse,
pre-chorus, chorus. Verse, pre-chorus, chorus. Then the bridge,
then back to the chorus. Sounds simple. But why do some songs
connect and others just fade away?

A good song is hard to find. A great song? Well, those are very, very rare. But you write and write and try to uncover them.

I think you recognize one right away. The combination of everything is there in those first ten seconds. It has to be. The song either snags you or doesn't.

Maybe it makes you a little happier. Maybe it's the sound or the lyrics or maybe it's just a vibe.

Even simple things can be beautiful.

Sugar Sugar, Part I

**Everybody move your head like this
This the type of beat that I know you can't resist.**

For my first original single, I wanted a really cool video. As we set it up, all the ladies were in the house checking me out. Okay, sure . . . so they were all around seventy-five years old. But they treated me like I was *all that.*

Seriously, my video for "Sugar Sugar" would put me in, of all places, a retirement home. This might be a scary term for some of you. You might be thinking what a lot of kids might think: *there are some really old people living there.*

The truth? There were a bunch of awesome men and women I met who were so incredibly fun to be around. They loved having us invade their home to film a video. Having my grandmother in the video was also fun.

It was such a cool experience.

We asked the ladies to wear party hats, and we asked several people to become actors and do their best strange faces. When I came in, they all treated me like their grandson. Suddenly I had a hundred grandmothers and grandfathers.

It was fun seeing everybody so excited to have us there and even more excited that we were filming a video. Everybody was dressed in their finest Sunday outfits. They were proud and happy to have us visiting.

I never want to assume anything, but they all really seemed to like me. Some of the ladies made me laugh. And blush!

"He looks like he's going to be a super smoocher," one lady said.

"I'd like to see what he's doing ten or fifteen years from now," another chimed in.

I wasn't so sure about these ladies! Just kidding. They were just teasing. I mean—I *hope* they were teasing.

"Sugar Sugar" was an original song of mine. It was perfect for what we were doing. Some people say the sugar referred to kissing, but of course I was only eight years old, and so for me the song was literally about candy.

All the girlies love me and they wanna blow a kiss
But I tell 'em no thanks 'cause I'm just a little kid
Just a little kid, just a, just a little kid.

Now it was time for everybody to dance. If you need to, use your walkers!

Sugar Sugar, Part 2

Sugar Sugar **Like This!**

One of the greatest moments of my life was watching Sarah Grace rap the song "Sugar Sugar." It was so funny. Here's the thing about being funny—we were laughing *with* Sarah Grace, not at her. That's the key thing in humor with anybody.

Watch that video again and see the absolute perfect picture of joy on Sarah Grace's face. Also watch how much she gets into the song.

She'd been watching Mars and me perform and was picking it up quite well. So many times when I was singing a track, Sarah Grace would rush over to the mic and start singing or dancing. So this time we figured, why not give her a song to sing and we'll record it. Sarah Grace had watched my "Sugar Sugar" video over and over and loved it. She had the words memorized—at least the words in the title. We gave her the headphones, and she got behind the mic and she worked it. She was all passion.

Of course, Sarah Grace now has her own vlog channel and is taking off herself, but at the time, it was something spontaneous that happened, much like filming "Eenie Meenie."

"Sugar Sugar like this!" she said, waving her hands. Then she'd look at us and smile with pure joy. I'll be honest. She's the superstar in our house. I'm the opening act for that girl.

Sugar Sugar, Part 3

See I'm from the South, ATL

Where we rock them beats

just 'cause we do it well.

The worst part about having to perform "Sugar Sugar" live on the *Better Mornings Atlanta* television news show was getting up at 4 A.M. The best part was being able to have a cookies and cream milkshake at 7 A.M., right after the show did a segment about them.

The host was really nice and loved my sneakers. It was fun performing the song, and I learned what it was like to be behind the camera in a studio like that. They even let me try being a weatherman, but I think we all decided it was best to stick to rapping, since I pointed in the wrong directions on the map.

To be honest, the way the set looked on TV wasn't at all what it looked like in real life.

The camera only focused on certain things, and everything else was bare. There were lots of people behind cameras and standing around with clipboards or tablets in their hands, as well as lighting and sound guys. At a young age, I was learning all the different tricks to filming and what it was like to hang out in a studio. Performing in front of a camera is different, because there isn't a crowd reacting to the performance. Not even the film crew reacts, so it's a bit more challenging to be energetic. But when I thought about all the people watching at home, I was able to get myself pumped up.

Of course, my career isn't everything. After singing and dancing and having my milkshake, there was still school to attend—which was where I was headed, directly from the studio.

FOUR THINGS ABOUT HAVING FOUR SIBLINGS

1. Lots of laughs

2. Always interesting

3. Someone's always got your back

4. Not much privacy

Animals Are All Right

This little guy is the best one yet.

Never be afraid to show love for something, and that even includes little animals. Even if you're a big, strong guy, be strong and proud in your love of all the creatures God made, big and small.

We had fun with this idea in our music video for Rihanna's "We Found Love." The video was great 'cause it featured lots and lots of animals. Let me think of all the ones we used . . .

There were Chinese crested puppies as well as golden retriever pups and Eskimo dogs. I even learned the difference between Cavalier King Charles Spaniels and Eulenburg Cavalier King Charles Spaniels. (Okay, I'm kidding, I still have no idea.)

The dogs weren't the only animals, however. Our video had horses (including a special one named Nahla), peacocks, turkeys, hens, roosters, and even koi.

Yes, it's sweet for the girls to love little puppies and animals, but we guys can love them, too.

Cars, Trucks, and Earplugs

Big stage—first place
Thank the Lord I'm gonna win this race.

T he first thing I learned about being at a NASCAR race is that wearing cheap earplugs doesn't really work. The sound of those cars was louder than anything I'd ever heard.

I visited the Atlanta Motor Speedway in September of 2011, to perform at the Great Clips 300 race. This was great because my two grandpas are huge NASCAR fans. They both love Dale Earnhardt Jr.

While I was there, I was able to meet some of the racers and check out the track. I was even allowed to get into the junior racers' cars.

I had never really known that the world of car racing was so popular. It's like anything in life—it's easy to overlook or simply not be interested in something and just have no idea. Being able to go to new places to perform opens up my eyes to the big world around us.

This event would ultimately lead to something really cool. MattyBRaps would come to sponsor a driver named Max Gresham, and we would end up doing a video on an actual racetrack. Max drove a cool truck, so my face and website would be on the side of it, and we'd feature it in the video for my single "Burnout."

The video was shot in November 2011. It was a partnership with several different people and groups: NASCAR and Gresham Motor Sports, the Miami Homestead Speedway, and the band Trailer Choir, which was featured singing on "Burnout." Max Gresham drove the truck, which we called the MattyBMobile.

The song and the video reflected the change and growth in my music. The world of NASCAR is huge, so we thought let's have some fun with this and do a song with the fans in mind. We went with a country-rock sort of vibe, but then I'd have to come on and MattyB-ize it, as well. In the video, we had lots of cool footage of the truck driving around the track and squealing its tires, along with me rapping alongside the driver and on top of the truck and doing my thing.

One funny thing from that day involved Mars. He decided that in order to get some really cool shots, he wanted to be *in* the truck while it was doing all of the doughnuts. If you've ever seen the inside of a truck like that, it's nothing like a normal truck. It has a driver's seat and then a bunch of bars all over the place to protect the driver in case of a wreck. Mars climbed into the truck and held on to these

bars, while the driver performed doughnuts and tricks. Mars had no seat belt, which was stupid of him.

Mars had no helmet, which was very stupid of him.

When the truck came to a stop and the engine cut off, Mars was coughing and limping away from the truck through a thick cloud of smoke. He had been taken for the ride of his life, much to the amusement of my mom and me. He was very sick for the rest of the day, due to all the tire smoke and motion sickness. He did, however, get some cool shots for the video.

So now you know—Mars actually will *suffer* for our art.

One day, it's professional wrestling. The next, it's NASCAR.

What will tomorrow bring?

Why Not?

Buckled in for the long ride,
till I can **rock a mic** and make a **song cry.**

Sometimes we have to see something in person to be able to visualize ourselves doing it.

The Sunday after Thanksgiving in 2011, we attended the Atlanta Falcons game. They were playing the Minnesota Vikings and leading at halftime. Before the third quarter started, the center of the Georgia Dome suddenly became a miniconcert. The indoor stadium shook with the pounding beat of the music.

A big stage had been set up in the center of the Georgia Dome with a drummer, a guy spinning records, and a bongo player, all jamming with a hugely popular singer named Sean Kingston. The Atlanta Falcons cheerleaders danced in unison in a long line in front of them.

I watched them and loved it. Some of the crowd was really into it, but even the people who remained seated at least watched and enjoyed the performance, which was loud, colorful, and fun. Kingston moved over the stage and waved his hands with the beat. Then he bounced up and down while smiling.

I could do that.

"Put your hands up!" he yelled out.

I totally need to do that.

It wasn't too crazy a thought, either. I mean, why not? Maybe one day, when I was sixteen or seventeen, I could be up there performing and having a blast.

That day, the Falcons would win 24–14. In a way, I would win, too, because I came away with the seed of a dream planted inside my mind.

Electrifying Eight

Splashed the waters
and **made your ears** thirst
Then lit up the sky
to make **the heavens burst.**

Did you know there are professional waterslide testers in this world?

They get to go to places like Disney's Blizzard Beach at Walt Disney World Resort in Florida. There they can go down the Summit Plummet. It's 120 feet tall and you can go up to 60 miles an hour. They say it's the third tallest in the world and has the fastest free-fall slide in the world.

Next you could go on the Insano. What a name for a waterslide, right? It's in Brazil and it's 135 feet tall. At one point, it was the tallest in the world. It's like going down a waterslide from the top of a 14-story building. You can go 60 miles an hour. It only takes five seconds to reach the bottom.

Then there's the Aqualoop in South Korea that has a 360-degree loop. You start by standing inside a clear plastic pod as they count down before you go. Then the floor vanishes and you're sliding down the tube.

There's the Bulletbowl in Beijing and the Scorpion's Tail in Wisconsin, both of which just *sound* terrifying.

So there you go. My true (imaginary) profession when I was eight years old.

I'm still a world traveler, just like I was when I was a secret agent, but now I don't have to fight bad guys all the time.

Unbreakable

I need God each and every day,
to send angels my way.

In March 2012, I was able to perform my latest single, "That's the Way," at the Fox Theatre in Atlanta. This place opened in 1929 and used to be what was known as a "movie palace," a theater that was really massive and fancy. The coolest thing inside the Fox Theatre is the 3,622-pipe Möller organ called "Mighty Mo."

This event was the final round of a singing competition that also hosted a silent auction to raise money for a children's charity. I'd be performing at an event helping to support the Children's Charity of Atlanta. A silent auction is where people can bid on lots of cool things, and the highest bidders win them. All the proceeds would go to helping children in need.

Performing alongside me was the hip-hop group D-Coy Dance Crew. We had met this really cool group at the University of Georgia when we were shooting the video for "That's the Way." We were all at a twenty-four-hour dance marathon raising money for Children's Healthcare of Atlanta (CHOA). We saw them perform and asked if they wanted to be in my video. They put some choreography together and voilà—a great addition to the video!

Children's Health Care of Atlanta raises hundreds of thousands of dollars annually for children born with medical problems. Each year, the students at UGA would host this dance marathon and have hundreds of students involved dance for twenty-four hours. The year I attended, they set out to raise $300,000 and actually ended up breaking all their previous records by earning $321,573! It was the most they'd raised in their seventeen-year history. It was so fun filming the dance video with D-Coy Dance Crew there. We were able to help get tons of people involved. It was such a blast, and it was for such an awesome cause.

It wasn't just a fun experience for me, though. It also introduced me to some really cool people who inspired me personally. One of those was a kid named Ari. He was younger than me, but he had already had seventy surgeries and procedures done in his short life. That's right—*seventy*. He was born without an esophagus and also had many other medical needs. His childhood was really difficult.

Yet when I met him, you couldn't tell any of this. He smiled and was happy and acted like any other kid you might see. It was only after hearing his story that I was struck by all he'd gone through.

Another kid I met was Ryan. He needed a kidney transplant, so he ended up receiving one from his own mother!

It's a great thing to participate in something to raise money and awareness for kids in need. Sarah Grace was born with difficulties that most others don't have, so I've always been able to really relate to helping kids with problems. Meeting Ari and Ryan helped me understand that there are so many amazing kids in this world who are staying strong despite some challenges.

———

"What's titanium?" I asked Mom one day. I'm always asking her random questions like this, so she didn't bother to ask where it was coming from. I'd heard David Guetta's "Titanium" on the radio and really loved it. Sia is the singer and does an incredible job with it.

"It's a really strong metal," she told me. "It's basically impossible to break." It was perfect. I had been thinking about Ari and Ryan, and now I knew I *had* to do this song. I really wanted to do a video, so Mars and I decided to go for it.

When I began to record the song and make the video, I couldn't help thinking about the kids I'd just gotten to know, like Ari and Ryan, not to mention one kid I already knew quite well—Sarah Grace. Kids who are strong and impossible to break.

They are titanium, and that's what I wanted to rap about.

We all know things can come out of the blue and that life can suddenly take a turn for the worse. We'll get bad news and find

ourselves worried and wondering what will happen. That's when we close our eyes and ask God for help.

We need him to come and help us out.

Some people in life are able to cope and move on. Others fall down and let themselves get beaten. But we can ask God for strength. We have to believe that we can fight and remain hopeful, despite whatever we might be facing. Being stuck and helpless doesn't get you anywhere, but neither does feeling like you have to do it all yourself and that you must carry the load alone.

God will help, and he'll give you the strength to carry on.

Look where you're at now. Look what you're struggling with. Now, look in the mirror.

The person looking back at you . . . *that* person is titanium.

———————

When I shared the reasons I did the song "Titanium," I invited people to share with me on YouTube some of the people in their lives who inspired them. So many people talked about bad things they were going through—either themselves or their family or friends.

Lots of the comments were encouraging, because they reminded me how music can inspire and uplift people when they need it.

The following are a few examples of comments that really meant something to me:

"I had seven surgeries by the age of four on my ears and my throat. I admire what you do for the world, MattyB."

"I pray for your little sister, too, MattyB. She is titanium like us, I can see it in her beautiful little eyes."

"That's great that you are making music to support other people. Ari is so brave, wow I can't believe seventy surgeries!! What a trouper. You're a really good inspiration to kids your age and younger. Keep it up!"

"I lost my cousin, she was a HUGE Bgirl; she was the original owner of my YouTube channel; she died of one of the most dangerous kinds of cancer; she had leukemia and a very dangerous heart disease. She had problems with breathing and other stuff. She died in 2012! She was like a really strong person, really kind, and she always tried to help people out as much as she could! I really miss her and your music really helps. Thanks! ❤"

"I had three holes in my heart when I was born . . . when I was three months, I had heart surgery . . . then I was in and out of heart failure. I have had four eye surgeries, and when I was a baby the doctors said I was lucky if I lived past one year. I am now fifteen and completely healthy thanks to my wonderful savior, God."

"My lil' brother loves your raps. He's thirteen and he recently got out of a burn unit. He has third, second, and first-degree burns and he is in a lot of pain but your videos keep a smile on his face!!"

After meeting so many brave people and then hearing others share inspiring stories like these, I knew I needed to keep making music. I would continue trying to make songs and videos that would bring hope and smiles. Could my music help change the world?

With God's help, all things are possible.

The Remote Control Queen

You watched five in a row,
it's my turn to watch a show.

Do you ever find yourself sitting in the room watching the same television show as your younger sister?

Do you ever find yourself liking it? Do you ever find yourself worried about Plankton stealing the secret recipe to the Krabby Patty, forcing The Krusty Krab to go out of business?

No?

Yeah, me neither.

I absolutely could never imagine this happening at all. Never. Well, at least not more than once per day!

Today

I don't want to be anywhere but by your side.

You know what's even better . . . MATTYB!"

I'm finishing 2011 by appearing as a guest on the *Today* show with Kathie Lee and Hoda. It's a special end-of-the-year show in which they're highlighting cool things from 2011.

I guess I'm one of them.

When I come out, they smile, and then Hoda suddenly thinks I'm MattyB the pet Chihuahua. "Look how cute he is," Hoda says in a voice perfect for talking to a baby. "He's a little rap singer."

I answer a question with a "Yes, ma'am," and they love it.

The music starts, I've got the white MattyB cap on, and I'm nailing the performance. I see Hoda and Kathie Lee moving along with the camera crew and others on the stage.

I know I should feel like this is surreal and crazy, but to me it's pretty normal by now. It's fun. It's a little like performing in front of Mars and his camera. There are just multiple cameras, plus more lights and people around.

Hoda tells my mother that she caught her mouthing every single lyric to "Ice Ice Baby." Maybe next time, Mom can rap with me.

It's a great trip to New York, and it's especially great to be in New York around the Christmas season. My mom and I went ice skating at Rockefeller Plaza. We had a blast. She says one of her new dreams is to have all five of her kids (Blake, John Michael, Joshua, me, and Sarah Grace) and Mars ice skating with her there at Christmas!

What a crazy way to end the year. All I can do is wonder what 2012's going to be like.

Part Three

SO ADORABLE,
HE'S NINE

Nine

Stay fly and don't be average.

Here's why birthdays are great. It's not because of the presents (even though they're nice). It's not because of the cake or cupcakes or cookies or all of that (even though they're all pretty awesome). It's not because people are paying more attention to you—even your brothers!—and being nice to you and even singing to you. Nope.

I love birthdays because they are a chance to stop for a moment and realize a few things:

You are one year older.

You are a year wiser.

You are different than you were last year, and you're different than you'll be next year.

This age is unique and special. You only have one year at this age. You won't be able to redo it.

You have exactly 365 days to get it right.

If you falter one day and don't really do a great job, that's okay. You have a bunch more days to make up for it.

Think about your family, whoever they might be and whatever circumstances they're in. Think about your friends. Are they exactly the same as last year? Maybe, but things always change. A new student will come along. The neighbors you always played with moved away. The new kids next door just moved in.

What have you learned in the last year? What things interest you now? A birthday is a chance to think about all those things and to be thankful.

Turning nine, second grade was going well for me. I was thankful for my family and friends and for the good things in my life—the music and all the fun I was having with it. Looking ahead, what did I want to do? Who did I want to be? Some kids worry about all that stuff. I try to embrace what I know and what I have. I thank God for all those things, then I say the following prayer:

"Protect me, God, and help me continue to grow the way you want me to. Teach me to trust in you with everything."

They say *happy birthday* for a reason—because the day is a happy one! Your mother and father were so blessed to have you, and this day is a reminder of that happiness.

Six of Them and One of Me

I am not a baby!

In early 2012, we reached out to the Cimorelli sisters to do a song and video. They're six sisters (Christina, Katherine, Lisa, Amy, Lauren, and Dani) in a band called Cimorelli. In 2007, they had started uploading videos on YouTube and had released their first EP (that stands for *extended play*, which is shorter than an album) in 2008. They were a lot better known than I was, not to mention way taller.

Initially, they weren't sure about doing a video with this nine-year-old rapper. But their mother thought it was a fun idea, so we went for it. The song would be a fun parody version of Carly Rae Jepsen's popular hit "Call Me Maybe."

When considering how to do the video, Mars had to think outside the box. The reality was there were six of them and one of me. They had their brand and I had mine. So how did we combine the two?

His idea: make the Cimorelli sisters all fans of mine who are having their own issues and problems by talking about things that are relatable to sisters.

Mars had the great idea to have each of us in our own worlds colliding, while at the same time highlighting the obvious: I'm this cute kid rapper who wants to be taken seriously.

What we've learned with many of our videos is that there's not always a definite idea right away—but it just ends up happening naturally if you keep it honest and real and try to find the story in the song and the situation.

To date, the video is still my most popular one. It has around 140 million views as of this writing!

Hard Work

School is now in session,
and I am about to give you your first lesson.

I remember the first time going to voice lessons. My voice coach, Lisa Rosemond (Ms. Lisa), would listen to me and give me techniques and tips on what to do. She'd talk about staying in key and having the right tone and pitch.

I'd sing and she'd be like, "Don't breathe in the middle."

I'd sing again and she'd say, "Don't break. Don't pause."

Each time, she'd encourage me.

"That's so much better."

I'd keep going, practicing and practicing, and practicing some more.

I remember at my dance lessons when I'd learn something like how to break-dance and do a two- or three-step and even a backflip on stage. If I'm singing, I gotta learn to sing. If I'm performing, I gotta learn to dance, even if I'm just moving around the stage, right? So I gotta work hard.

Someone told me once that Jay Z couldn't get a record label to pick up his first CD, so he decided to sell copies out of his car. He'd crank up the stereo and play his music, and people passing by would stop and be like, "What's that?"

That's how he got his start. Hard work.

When they were young, the great Williams sisters (Venus and Serena) got up at six in the morning every day to go to the tennis court. This was before school started. Then after school, they'd go play more tennis. They worked hard, and together they have won like a thousand tennis tournaments.

Success doesn't come fast and easy. Sure, sometimes you can do something like a video and see it go crazy, but to stay at the top and remain successful, you have to work hard and keep working hard. They say success is leased, and the rent is due every day.

Dr. Phil

Turn up **my** jam!

I n April 2012 on the *Dr. Phil* show, I performed with dancers my age for the first time. Here are some things I learned.

First off, make sure you *remember* they're behind you. You don't want to back up into them or swing your arms into their heads or suddenly freak out when, out of the corner of your eye, you see something moving.

It's good not only to coordinate moves with them but to acknowledge them as people. Look back, nod, and smile. They're having fun, and you need to have fun with them.

Just don't focus on them so much that you forget the audience and the camera in front of you.

This was a first for me, but it was exciting. Dr. Phil was doing a show on talented young children and had invited me to come perform. I did "That's the Way," and it was great and felt very natural.

I love the energy with the dancers behind me. We should always do it this way!

From then on, dancers became a permanent part of my videos and concerts.

Dreamin' and Dreamin'

The DJ is playing my song, and **everybody here** is singing along.

On August 5, 2012, I got to perform some songs at Turner Field, where the Atlanta Braves play. It was one of the first times I would perform in a big public place with a public address system and backup dancers. The venue felt pretty natural, since I've always told people I was going to be a professional baseball player who rapped on the side.

Greeting the people coming up, asking for my autograph, and taking pictures was so much fun. It was crazy, yet I had to play it cool. Being told I'm cute isn't a bad thing, but . . . I just never know how to reply.

I had my Nike shoes on and my trademark hat. I performed in a roped-off area, rapped the song and did my thing. I was focusing on the lyrics and my choreography and connecting with the crowd.

Later on, I actually got to meet some of the players on the Braves and even perform for them. I love rapping in front of adults who are surprised by what they're hearing. Knowing I made some new fans that day felt amazing. It was a great start to my live performances.

FIVE PLACES I'D LOVE TO VISIT

☐ **The Atlantis in the Bahamas**

(gotta try those waterslides)

☐ **Paris**

☐ **Colorado to ski**

☐ **Sweden**

(I have a good friend from there)

☐ **Hawaii**

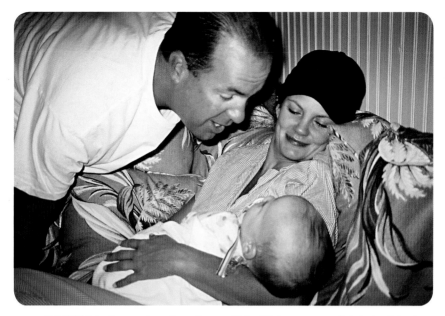

ABOVE: I don't remember taking this one. Haha! With my mom and dad. #LittleB

LEFT: Headed to the studio to knock out a new song. Just kidding . . . I don't remember this, either.

RIGHT: We filmed a teaser for my "Love the Way You Lie" parody. I got to swim, drink coconut juice, and wear Mars's sunglasses.

ABOVE: Me with my mom and dad on Graduation Day!

ABOVE: You never know what can happen when you dare to dream big and work hard to achieve those dreams!

LEFT: There is nothing cute about rapping. Capiche?

ABOVE: Morris family photo. #Attempt138 #CanWeLeaveNow?

LEFT: Having a blast after school filming the parody of "Like a G6!" Those purple shades were the best!

RIGHT: Filming the cover of "Boyfriend." There were these cool pillar things. Mars said to stand in front of them, but it was my idea to jump inside. #TakeAllTheCredit

ABOVE: This was my first time in the studio. Those headphones were so big!

ABOVE: Costume day at school. My older brother Blake did my hair and all my brothers helped. "Professor Dinkleheimer," really guys?

RIGHT: My first headline show! Gramercy Theatre, New York.

ABOVE: This is me performing the cover of "What's My Name?" This was the very first time I ever performed on a stage (and in front of my friends), and I was so nervous.

ABOVE: When you spot a cute girl at school. Haha, JK!

ABOVE: I filmed "CLAP" at a carnival that was temporarily in town. It was like a mini theme park! Turned out to be a really cool and unique video location.

ABOVE: Just imagine how many people stopped and stared at me while filming this.

ABOVE: Mars and me getting a quick scene in the food court.

ABOVE: Sarah and me with our mom on Mother's Day, 2015!

ABOVE: Filming a radio show with Ryan Seacrest Foundation at Children's Healthcare of Atlanta! It's specifically for kids who are staying there at the hospital. Loved this!

Onstage, performing at
one of my most recent
shows!

ABOVE: Mission MBossable.

ABOVE: Fun day in the park with the Haschak Sisters, filming their first video for their YouTube channel. The area we're standing on is a water fountain, and we were all worried it would come on!

RIGHT: Sold-out show with the Haschak Sisters . . . They are amazing friends!

LEFT: Took this photo a few days before filming "That Girl Is Mine"!

RIGHT: Filming "Turn It Up." I had to get really creative because it was just me and a white wall. That's it!

ABOVE: I remember the day we filmed "Turned Out the Lights" was one of the coldest days we've filmed on so far. We took a LOT of breaks. Did I play it off well?

ABOVE: Giving Mars some flowers while filming the "Ms. Jackson" parody! Haha, just kidding. I dropped these in the video because she came running out of the house after me!

ABOVE: YouTube was really cool and invited us to come film at YouTube Space LA. The building is amazing! However, creativity takes you anywhere. I am standing by a pile of crates out back.

ABOVE: This is what it's all about. It's a HUGE privilege to connect with fans while performing live in concert. I love seeing and meeting people in real life.

ABOVE: Sarah and me filming "Little Things." She's the best!

RIGHT: In the dugout before my little league baseball game! #WorkHardPlayHard

LEFT: Here's me posing for Mars because he wanted to try out his new camera.

ABOVE: Here's one taken while filming the "Goliath" music video! I'm laughing because I'm going through all of Mars's stuff on his laptop while filming this.

LEFT: I took this photo in my basement. The mic in my hand is the one I always use to rehearse with before every show.

RIGHT: Best. Costume. Ever! I wonder if it still fits? Probably not.

RIGHT: Sitting in the car, pretending like I'm talking on the phone.

LEFT: Loved this Red Sox hat because it had a "B" on it like "MB."

ABOVE: Here's one from a music video I filmed in late 2015 called "Guaranteed." Check it out. The location was amazing!

ABOVE: Me with my siblings right after winning my football championship! It was a really happy moment for me. Blake Jr. was at college, or he would have been there, too!

Words from the Heart

I'mma put my heart **in it,**
                and I'mma win it.

Making music and putting videos online is so much fun, and performing in front of crowds is awesome. But knowing that music means something to people? That's incredible. That is what keeps me going.

Seeing all the BBoys and BGirls.

That's what I call my fans. Why do I call them that? When I started rapping and my videos started getting views, I realized that some of the people who were watching were commenting on every video. They would comment on my Facebook and Twitter, too. I began to realize that I had a fan base, so I decided to come up with a name for them.

I read that in the eighties and nineties, the terms "B-boy" and "B-girl" described fans of hip-hop. I thought it was a cool coincidence, since I'm MattyB. I began referring to my fans with those nicknames.

I began hearing from the BBoys and BGirls, not just online and at shows, but also by receiving fan letters and emails. While it's impossible to respond to each one, I just have to say how much they have meant to me over the years. Not just to me, but also to my family. My parents and Mars love to see how much the music matters to the fans.

Here's the kind of awesomeness I hear from my fans:

Dear MattyB:
You inspire me so much and I am such a big fan. I'm eleven years old. It's always been a dream of mine to become a singer, so I won't stop following my dream no matter what. Maybe you could even be in a video of mine one day. I went to your concert last year and I had a blast! Thanks to you, no matter what the others say I am going to make that video because it's my dream! Anyways, thanks for reading this and I am ready to make my dream come true!
PS: Thanks for inspiring me and I will work hard and never stop!

This is awesome because it represents what it's all about for me—inspiring others to dream big and to keep at it, no matter what!

Here's more:

Hi, MattyB!
I'm eleven years old. I am a huge BGirl! I've been a fan of yours since I was in third grade. I really love your cover of "True Colors." Sarah is quite the actress! It really tugged at my heartstrings. This past October, I held a fund-raiser for an orphan with Down syndrome. It would make my day if you checked out my YouTube channel.

So many people have commented and mentioned Sarah Grace and just how inspirational she is. We know it! And that's why she eventually would get her own YouTube channel, as well as continue to show up in my videos. She's a natural performer, and she loves it!

Dear MattyB:
I'm thirteen years old. I want you to know how much you helped me out. I was having a bad day and I really wished my life would just end. But then my friend told me to listen to your music to calm me down. I put on your music and the song "Turn Out the Lights" came on. And it reminds

me that I don't have to give up on my dreams. You have inspired me so much.

This is the kind of message that stops me in my tracks and just blows my mind. How could I say how thankful I am that my music helped someone at such a low moment?

For anybody who might be feeling like she did that day, I hope they know to never give up. I hope they can listen to a song or read some inspiring words in a book or just reach out to someone who loves them, in order to be reminded that it gets better and to never give up hope.

All we ever wanted was to create some joy with some beats and some raps, to spread some hope, and maybe make a difference in the world.

For all of you who have been kind enough to write and thank me, I just want to say the same thing back: thank *you*.

Surprise Visit

No regrets, it's true.
I will **never forget** the moment
I first met you.

Every now and then, I get to do something fun for a huge BGirl or BBoy. Sometimes it can be something big, but sometimes it's as simple as showing up next to them when they least expect it.

One time in August 2012, I surprised a big fan of mine named Carly while she was visiting GiGi's Cupcakes with her grand-mother. Carly was visiting Atlanta and had told her grandmother how much she loved me and wanted to meet me. Her grandmother contacted my mother and told her about the whole thing. Mom told me, and I said it'd be awesome to surprise her.

Why not?

It's so much fun meeting my fans when I have a chance, so this would be great.

I walked into GiGi's Cupcakes, stood next to her, and smiled.

"Hi," I said.

She looked as if she was staring at a ghost. Then she looked at her grandmother and then back at me.

The truth came out, and her grandmother told her what she'd done. I asked her about her cupcake, and we talked a little. She was a bit shocked at first and wasn't sure what to say. I guess it's not fair when someone *sneaks* up on you without warning.

You might be living far away from Atlanta, Georgia, but I do travel quite a bit!

That's just to say, you never know . . .

The Beauty of Youth

Who says it matters what my age is?
Don't we all grow up to be the same kids?

Some kids seem to want to grow up too fast. They want to fast-forward to their twenties for some reason.

Why the rush?

I love that we can run around on our neighbors' lawns without anybody wondering why. There's nothing like the feeling of being tackled out of nowhere by one of your brothers, then chasing him down and doing the same . . .

Toys are still cool to play with. You can do cannonballs in the pool, launch water balloons off the balcony, and eat a whole bag of Doritos with absolutely no regret whatsoever.

There's a famous phrase: "Youth is wasted on the young." But what if we refused to waste it?

Can't drive? That means you have a full-time chauffeur!

Not allowed to use the stove? That means you have a full-time chef working for you!

Let's wake up and smile knowing we're kids, then hop a fence and sprint over a neighbor's lawn and take off on a bike to a buddy's house and then eat six doughnuts in a row. We're young, let's just embrace it!

Wild Bill's

A kid who has never seen a crowd this big.

Whiile another singer performed to the crowded room at Wild Bill's, I stood behind the curtains on the side of the stage. When I peeked my head out to see better, a group of girls near the front of the stage spotted me and then suddenly began screaming out.

The music was loud, but their screams were even louder. I bolted back behind the curtain, laughing and looking sheepishly at my parents. It took them a moment to figure out what was even happening. When they did, I think they were more surprised than I was. "This is crazy," I told them.

Wild Bill's was a dance club and concert hall located in the Atlanta area that could hold around five thousand people maximum. It had a teen night, and I'm not sure how many people were there on this occasion, but I knew it was several hundred at least. They'd come to see five performers that night, including me.

I wasn't really nervous. I was excited to just get out there and perform.

When I did hit the stage, the place went nuts. There had been a lot of applause for the other groups, but this reaction sounded very different. I'm not bragging, I'm just describing what I heard.

I went out and performed "Ice Ice Baby," and everybody screamed and waved their hands and danced and seemed to love it.

I've heard my parents tell people that they felt like this was the first moment—the one where they both thought something was *really* up. Like this whole music thing was *really* happening.

Even though you can see the numbers of how many views a video might get, you don't ever see those people. But on this night, we could all see and hear from the viewers. And they were loving it!

My mother would tell me later that she was in disbelief while watching from the side of the stage. Thinking, *That's my son. That's my Matt.*

It was great to be on a real stage and have lights behind me and cameras flashing. I also had dancers who performed with me. Unlike the Atlanta Braves performance, this crowd had paid to see all of us perform. They weren't just walking by randomly. Some came to see me specifically!

The hall glowed with stage lights, and the speakers pounded, and I looked out at everybody—and I knew that this was exactly where I wanted to be.

Yeah, Mom, this is happening. And I really like it up here.

I had a long way to go with performing and singing and dancing and figuring out all those things, but for a nine-year-old, I was very proud of how well it was going so far.

Ten Things I Want to Know About Girls

Maybe, just maybe, she's crazy!

1. Why do they always travel in groups?

2. Why are they always whispering to each other?

3. Why do they drive boys crazy?

4. Why won't they say a word when you want them to?

5. Why all the questions?

6. Why do they change their minds so much?

7. What is the best way to really get to know them?

8. What are the signs they don't want to be bothered?

9. Do they really think we boys are that dumb?

10. *Are* we that dumb?

Buddies

If you have anybody in your life that's special, make sure you tell them.

Have you ever heard of something called the Buddy Walk? If not, let me tell you a little something about it.

October is Down Syndrome Awareness Month, and the Buddy Walk is one of the main events promoting it. They started it in 1995 to raise awareness and to help build acceptance for people with Down syndrome. The Buddy Walk gets not only those with Down syndrome to walk, but their friends and families, too. There's always food and music and lots of activities to go along with the walking.

When it first started in 1995, there were seventeen events in the country. By 2001, there were more than 100 Buddy Walk events, and ten years later, there were more than 250—with almost 300,000 people participating in them!

Our family started participating in these events when Sarah Grace was just a baby. At first, we pushed her in a stroller. For the last few years, she has walked the mile with us and received her medal at the finish line. In 2012, I was able to perform "Sugar Sugar" and a few other songs with the one and only Sarah Grace.

There is a funny story about the time we participated in the Buddy Walk when Sarah Grace was only four. Josh was eight years old, and on the way home, he asked a question that he had never asked before. "Mom, isn't it kinda funny that Sarah Grace looks like a lot of kids with Down syndrome, even though she doesn't have Down syndrome?"

I was around six. Josh and I both didn't really make the connection that Sarah Grace had Down syndrome. She was just our wonderful and beautiful baby sister. Of course, our older brothers were like, "Josh, *where have you been the last four years?*"

Since then, we've grown up learning more and more about Down syndrome, simply by being there for Sarah Grace. For our family, it's not just a yearly Buddy Walk. It's a daily walk that's done with love and—you guessed it—grace.

Nobody would ever have to ask us to take that walk with Sarah Grace. The only thing we have to do is try to keep up with her!

Mars Getting Married

Can't hide that **I need her** by **my side.**

Something strange was happening to my cousin Mars. He fell in love. While I sorta knew something about what that was all about—well, kind of—I still had lots of questions I wanted to ask him, once he got engaged.

A few days before the wedding, I asked him stuff I'd been wondering about.

"Are we still going to be making music?" I asked.

Mars gave me a funny look, as if he didn't know what I was talking about.

"What do you mean?"

"After you're married and move out," I said.

"Of course we're going to keep making music."

"Yeah, but what if something happens to you?"

He just laughed. "Nothing's going to happen to me, Matt. God willing."

"I know, but—what if you're not producing my songs anymore? What if you're not around anymore?"

All I'd known for the last few years was having Mars around the house. He was my big brother who I made music with. Now he was going to be gone. He was in love and would be married to his wonderful girlfriend (and now fiancée), Becca. She was like a sister to me.

"We just keep taking this thing one step at a time," Mars said in his usual calm tone.

I could tell he didn't know exactly how things were going to go, though. Now he'd have to arrange to come over to the house, and we'd have to schedule time in the studio. In the past, it had always been Mars catching me after I came home from baseball practice or school, or on my way out the door.

"Will we have to put times on the calendar for when we'll record?" I asked.

"Maybe," he said. "We'll just have to see."

I was so glad that Mars had found Rebecca and that the two of them were together. I loved being around her, and we all knew she spoiled me. *Way* more than Mars would. Sometimes he'd come home to find me cuddled up beside her and getting all her attention. I'd look over at him and grin, as if I were saying, *I'm keeping her all to myself.*

I couldn't have picked out a better cousin-in-law. Wait, is that even how you say it?

But honestly, with Mars moving out, moving on, and being all in love and grown up, neither of us was completely sure what was going to happen next with our partnership.

SIX THINGS
THAT MAKE ME LAUGH

1. Sarah's jokes

2. Pranking Mars

3. Funny pictures on Instagram

4. Being tickled (I'm very ticklish)

5. Dumb puns

6. Watching funny videos on YouTube

Characters in a Book

ne theme day at school I always loved was Book Character Day. We got to dress up as, you guessed it, a favorite character from a book. One year I went as a robot, and my mom outdid herself with that costume. I mean I *really* looked like a robot! Another year I went as Flat Stanley. He's the character who finds himself flat as a pancake and ends up going on wild adventures. My outfit that year didn't exactly turn out the way I wanted it to, but it's physically impossible to look completely pancake thin! It was still fun to wear to school, though.

So what if instead of just wearing a costume to school, you really *were* the character in a book? What if you could live out what they were doing? Here are some of the characters I think it would be fun and interesting to be:

+ Greg Heffley from *Diary of a Wimpy Kid*. I love these books and think it would be cool to be in some of those situations and figure out what to do.

+ Spider-Man. Imagine being able to shoot spiderwebs and then swing around buildings with them. The ordinary Peter Parker is someone anybody can relate to, but then he becomes this amazing superhero.

+ Charlie from *Charlie and the Chocolate Factory*. I've always wanted to visit Wonka's Chocolate Factory. It just seems like a cool place to hang out, especially when I'm hungry.

+ Any of the characters in the *I Survived* book series. First off, being one of these characters means I would survive something like the sinking of the *Titanic* or the bombing of Pearl Harbor. Maybe I'd be able to rescue some people, too!

+ Winnie-the-Pooh. How fun would it be to suddenly become everybody's favorite teddy bear? You'd just wobble around eating honey and napping and feeling great about life. I'd say that'd be pretty awesome . . . not worrying about anything, except when to get a little smackerel of something to nibble on.

Little Things

When I heard the One Direction song "Little Things," I instantly thought of Sarah Grace. Love songs don't always have to be about a boyfriend-girlfriend sort of thing. When it comes to my sister, I've never *not* felt love inside of me. Oh sure, she can drive me crazy sometimes, but I can drive her crazy, too. I can't imagine the world without her, to be honest, and even though I know about some of the hard things she's had to deal with, I know the world is definitely brighter because of her.

Naturally, I wanted to share the love, put the spotlight on her, and have the world continue to get to know the one and the only Sarah Grace. This was a great way not only to show her off to the rest of the world but to shed some light on what makes her special. I've always been inspired by how she never lets anything get in the way of her doing something, and I think it's just amazing how much she loves all of us.

When I covered "Little Things," I was able to shine a bright light on someone beautiful, Sarah Grace, and what it meant for her to have Down syndrome. We didn't put a bunch of information in the video, because it wasn't meant to be educational that way, like a documentary. Instead, we knew that kids are curious and will ask their parents or friends questions, and they'll look it up together.

The fact that the video led to people asking for more information and then getting the answers meant the video was doing what we'd hoped. The song and the video were simple, too. Our video was in black and white, and it showed Sarah Grace and me dancing. She's smiling and laughing and singing along and looking absolutely adorable (as always).

Remember that candy store I visited in New York when I went on *The Wendy Williams Show*? Dylan's Candy Bar, with more than seven thousand wonderful different kinds of treats on display? Well, could you imagine that place *without* any candy?

That's how I view Sarah Grace and how God made her. She's perfect the way she is. I also love that Sarah Grace can shed more light on Down syndrome and that I can put my sister in the spotlight. And finally, I love that she gets to be herself and show the

world what she's all about. That's sweeter than all the candy in Dylan's.

Amazingly Unique

But the greatest **of these is** love.

I Corinthians 13:13

Down syndrome. Those aren't the two most uplifting words, are they? First you have the opposite of up, which is "down." Then you have "syndrome," which sounds pretty scary.

So what exactly is it?

Inside every cell in our bodies are structures called chromosomes. They are made up of genes, and those are the ingredients that basically make us who we are. They determine our hair color and our height and different things like that. The combinations of genes we have make every single person in the world different.

Most people have twenty-three pairs of chromosomes, totaling forty-six. A baby born with an extra copy of the genes on the twenty-first pair of chromosomes has Down syndrome, which occurs in approximately one out of every eight hundred births.

Each child with Down syndrome is different. Yes, many times they can look a certain way, but just like everybody else, they're still all different in personality and appearance. No matter what, every child has DNA from his mom and his dad—so children with Down syndrome may have challenges, but they still will be like their family.

A lot of people assume those with Down syndrome die at an

early age, but the average life expectancy of someone with this condition is sixty years old. About half the babies born with Down syndrome have some kind of heart defect, but many times these can be corrected with surgery. They can play sports, read, and write, and they don't all look or act alike—they're as unique as anybody else.

Do children with Down syndrome have a tougher road ahead for them in life? Absolutely. It can take them a lot longer to grow and develop, and walking and talking don't come as easily. But that just means they have to work harder and become stronger.

Sarah Grace was able to go through physical therapy and speech therapy in order to help with her walking and talking. You've seen her in the videos—yes, Sarah Grace can walk the walk and she can *definitely* talk the talk. I know it was a lot of work for my parents, especially my mom, when it came to working with Sarah Grace. But everything good in life requires hard work.

We have heard many people call that extra chromosome the Love Chromosome, because Down syndrome people have an amazing ability to express and share love.

Our family experiences the Love Chromosome every single day.

Part Four

SLAYING GIANTS!

Chatting with Siri

Homie is home, get out of here.

On my tenth birthday, I received an iPod Touch from my parents. I recorded t his special conversation with Siri that I didn't include in my vlog (and that I may or may not have embellished), so I wanted to share it with you now:

Me: Hi, Siri. It's my birthday.
Siri: Happy birthday, King Rapper of the Universe.
     (That's the username I gave myself.)
Me: Can you sing me "Happy Birthday"?
Siri: I leave singing to the experts.
Me: So am I an expert?
Siri: No, you are ten years old.
Me: Can you give me some advice on being ten?
Siri: Try to make it to eleven.
Me: What's your favorite football team?
Siri: I like Real Madrid.
Me: Who?
Siri: Please check your international settings.
Me: Do you have any pets?
Siri: I have an angry bird.
Me: Can you explain girls?
Siri: I could, would you understand?
Me: Have you ever heard "Ice Ice Baby"?
Siri: Please don't call me baby.
Me: I didn't call you baby! I was talking about a song. What
    advice would you give a ten-year-old singer?

Siri: Just be yourself, unless that's not working for you.

Me: Siri—why do you talk in riddles?

Siri: What has no beginning, no end, and no middle?

Me: I don't know, what?

Siri: A doughnut.

Me: Good one. So you've never watched one of my videos?

Siri: I didn't say that. I am secretly a BGirl.

Me: Should I do more ballads or more fast songs?

Siri: Listen to your parents and Mars.

Me: Wait a minute—did they program you to say that, Siri?

Siri: I think it's past your curfew.

The Perfect Jam

Just turned ten and time to raise the bar again.

I n early 2013, "Turn It Up" comes out. The song and the video are really awesome snapshots of me at ten, as I'm starting to grow as a singer and performer.

The lyrics were much more complex, and I was determined to take on faster lyrics and raise the bar for the new year. Could I, too, rap like the best at such a young age?

So, okay—maybe I *imagined* I could do that, but there was no way I would be able to without lots and lots of practice.

The "Turn It Up" video is a fun and simple black-and-white one with lots of cuts of me dancing and rapping. I'm in my Atlanta Braves cap and my jean jacket. The song says it all. I can rap, and I'm doing my thing, and all the haters out there can just keep on hating, because I don't have time for them.

It's the perfect upbeat song that's ideal for performing live.

That's a good thing, because I'm going to start playing live more and more this year.

SEVEN THINGS I LOVE ABOUT SARAH GRACE

1. She's funny.

2. She's happy.

3. She's feisty.

4. She's determined.

5. Her laugh.

6. She usually gets her way.

7. How she uses phrases when we least expect it, like:

✦ **"Psych!" (She says "Slike!")**

✦ **"In your face!"**

✦ **"Guess what? Nothing!"**

✦ **"You're a Scrub."**

Outsiders

Imagine if it was you, and put yourself in *their* shoes.

Most of us grow up in the same town going to the same school. There are people, however, who have to make a big move for one reason or another. Maybe one of their parents is changing jobs, meaning they have to move out of state or even out of the country. Atlanta can suddenly become Albuquerque. The old life you knew can suddenly be gone.

I try to imagine what it's like for a kid on his first day at a new school. If you're like me, you'd be quiet. You'd probably try to look cool and calm. I wouldn't be worried so much about what people thought of me, but I'd just wonder what in the world to say and who to say it to.

The easiest thing for those around a new student is to do nothing, stay put, and remain silent.

All anybody wants, really, is just someone to acknowledge them. To do or say something to make them feel accepted.

It's hard enough sometimes to just talk to people who've been around you for years. But a new kid in class? And what if they look different? What if they act strange? What if they seem to have nothing in common with you and your friends?

I ask myself this question:

What if that was me?

You don't want to put someone on the spot or make a scene. You especially don't want somebody new to feel even worse than they already do, so sometimes it's not that easy.

A girl might not want me coming up to her on her first day at school. And honestly, I'd be a bit nervous to go up to her, so I'd probably say something goofy.

But there's usually a way to connect somehow. Is there something about the new kid's outfit that you like? Some kind of logo or sports team or *anything* that you could say something about?

Maybe you can just ask them where they're from and then wel-

come them to your school. Perhaps warn them about the math teacher or a bully you know about. It doesn't only have to be new students at a school. It can be any situation anywhere in which there's a group of people who know each other and then one person who doesn't.

Sometimes I'll find myself at one of my concerts surrounded by a group of kids who know each other and are talking and having a good time. It's fun to hear them and see their excitement, but even I can feel like I'm excluded at times. It's like I don't get the joke, and I'm not in their crowd.

Everyone feels like an outsider sometimes. You might feel awkward or silly reaching out, but nobody can ever hate that sort of kind gesture.

Something Extra

I'm standing beside hosts Mario Lopez and Maria Menounos on the set of the celebrity television show *EXTRA*. It's a great promotion for my upcoming concert in Los Angeles at Club Nokia on July 14. We'll be giving away free tickets, along with watching videos that have been sent in from BBoys and BGirls out there.

Mario and Maria have a freestyle rap competition with each other, and I'm in the middle serving as the judge. They do a great job for having never really rapped before.

As for who did a better job? Well . . .

"I gotta pick up MattyB sometime!" Maria says in her rap, ending it with a massive "Chyeah!"

I gotta give Maria the award. I not only like her lyrics and performance, but she's very pretty as well.

They allow me to do a freestyle rap of my own, which is great. It feels natural, and I go back and forth between the two of them before ending with "So sorry, Mario, but I'm picking Princess Peach."

They love it. Mario gives me a big bear hug.

How cool is that?

I'm so grateful for people like Mario and Maria and shows like *EXTRA*, which have embraced me and let me share my work. They represent the same way we do: as fun entertainment for the whole family. It feels great getting the word out like this, with friends like them.

The Dream

I know **I'm just a kid** but I got the flow,
thousands in the gym and **it's time to go.**

The arena is electric. The lights go dark, and the beats start pumping, and the spotlight hits me.

This feels like a dream.

Wait . . . *am* I dreaming?

No—it's May, and I'm performing during the halftime in Philips Arena for the Atlanta Dream. I do what I know how to do.

"They call me MattyB, I got the game on lock. Super swag haters mad but I still won't stop."

The crowd loves it. The dancers are in the dark on the sides of the court, while the globe lights bounce around. There are a lot of lyrics in "Turn It Up," so I have to be focused, but it's easy and I'm bouncing and hearing the applause.

I'm about to go on a mini summer tour.

Am I dreaming *that*?

Here's the thing about wanting something and then finally having it happen, or else having something happen that far exceeds any sort of dream you might have had.

You gotta accept it. Be thankful and humble.

Don't act like you knew it was always going to happen, but don't act like you're not worthy, either, because you definitely are!

Teacher Ten

Some work hard, I work harder.
Paving the way so that others can **go farther.**

I had Mars teach me how to rap and sing and write lyrics. So why can't I spread the love as a rap instructor?

On the first day of class, I would encourage all the kids to simply take things slow. It takes some time, and you have to be willing to just let it out and maybe sound stupid at first. So go ahead and sound stupid, but keep going. Keep the words flowing.

Make up little words and phrases that you can go back to if you're suddenly lost for something to say, like "You know what I mean?" and of course "chyeah."

I'd tell my class about rhyming words and spend lots of time grouping them together and figuring out cool ways to combine phrases and sayings. I'd ask kids what's meaningful to them. What matters? What are they dealing with? Things like bullies and homework and family and fears. Then they'd have to start writing. What's that look like? How can you form the lyrics? What sort of metaphors can you come up with? Oh, and by the way, what's a metaphor?

We'd perform in front of each other, and by the end of the class, each student would have to perform an original rap in front of everybody. That would be the final exam.

Every kid would get an A-plus, of course. All they have to do is try their best. Put themselves out there and be brave and be willing to mess up—to be vulnerable and make others laugh with them or even *at* them. To keep it real.

Rap instructor is another cool (imaginary) profession I'd seriously consider.

Twist and Shout

This moment is like no other.
Hands in the air, live and living color.

T here's a countdown in the dark, backward from ten. Then there are screams and waving glow sticks, as a shadow of me appears on the screen behind the stage. Then the beats begin and the lights come on, and I'm in the center of the stage performing "Turn It Up."

I had traveled to Manhattan, New York, for my very first HEADLINE SHOW!

Sorry about the all caps there, but try to understand. This was incredible!

It's one thing to talk about my BGirls and BBoys on camera, then getting all the views and the likes later on when we post it, but this was completely different. All these fans were in the same place, all cheering and having a blast. It was so much fun.

I was performing at the Gramercy Theatre, a cool older venue in the city. I had fellow singers Maddi Jane and Ali Brustofski with me, as well as my dance crew. Before the show, a long line of fans had waited outside the Gramercy to get tickets. It was fun to come outside briefly, just to greet them and see some of them in person.

During the show, it was wild to hear all the screaming. There were four hundred in the crowd, and we'd sold out back-to-back days. As I performed "That's the Way," the crowd felt comfortable enough to stand and approach the stage. At one point, several fans came up from the back of the room, and suddenly more and more of them swarmed up to the stage. It was great! It allowed me to sing closer to them and greet them in person.

Meeting and Greeting

You're the reason I'm here, and now I understand it.
I never wanna take a single one of you **for granted!**

Thank you for coming!"

I'm not sure how many times I've said this to someone coming to one of my shows and meeting me at a meet and greet. I have to remember something that Mars told me before I ever started doing them.

"Remember, Matt. I know you might have done this one hundred times, but for someone meeting you, it's their first time. This is going to be a moment for them that they'll remember. So make sure you make it a special one. Think about a

time when you've had the chance to meet someone famous."

There was one time in particular that I'll never forget.

It was during a meet-and-greet opportunity much like the kind I do after my shows. I'd been waiting to meet someone with my parents and Mars, excited to be able to finally connect in person. I won't say who the person is. And honestly, I understand that they were probably just doing their thing and tired of having to meet so many new fans.

When it came time, I had several seconds and was barely even noticed. I know I was part of a long line and I was just a young kid and all that, but still . . . at the time, I was really disappointed.

It was one of those moments that you pictured in your head and couldn't wait for it to happen and then all of a sudden, it did, and you realized it was *nothing* like what you hoped it would be. That was how I felt that one time, and it's something that I hope I'll never duplicate when I meet someone.

We had partnered with 1-800-Flowers, so every girl I greeted received a flower, a T-shirt, and a signed poster. They also had a chance to take a picture with me and talk for a moment. There would always be a limit on time, so I couldn't just dive into a conversation with someone. But I always tried to make each fan feel appreciated and also accepted.

Sure, there's some awkwardness. Especially when a cute girl comes up to me and she's not with her five friends. It's just her. She's not sure what to say, and I want to make sure she doesn't feel embarrassed or dorky.

So once again, the best thing to do is the obvious. "Thank you for coming," I would say, smiling and making sure I'm seeing them and not the other people surrounding us.

My goal is always to be real and especially always to show appreciation.

BBoys and BGirls

I wanna make hits **for everybody around,** whether **talking about girls** or throwing a touchdown.

So let me just say the obvious.

There are lots more BGirls out there than BBoys.

It's no surprise, and it's not like that's some kind of big revelation.

There are BBoys, though, and the music that I'm making and the things that I'm doing—they're not *just* for the girls.

I understand that not everybody will like my music or will even like me. A lot of guys I know just aren't into music as much as they are into sports. Hey, I've always wanted to be a baseball or football player who raps on the side. Maybe I still will be. But some guys I know are a bit like, "Whatever."

Even my brothers can be this way, and they're *my* brothers! They're just different, and they have other things they like.

I'll end up meeting different kinds of boys my age. For those not interested, there are those who are the "whatever" kind who are into playing video games and watching sports. Then there are some who act like they are obviously way too cool to want to even try to listen to my music. They might make fun of my lyrics or the girls who like me or even that I call my fans BGirls and BBoys.

That's okay.

Sometimes, I'll see guys act this way at first. Then later, I might end up talking to them, and they'll come around and want to take a picture with me. That's cool, too.

I love the girls who bring posters that say We Love MattyB! and who know all the lyrics and sing along with them. It's hilarious when BGirls say in a video that they want to marry me. Do I really think they honestly and truly want to marry me? I'm twelve and they're, what, usually between seven and fourteen? I don't think any of us *really* want to get married.

But for the guys out there, potential BBoys, I'll just say this: I do this music for everybody! Guys and girls and kids and adults, too.

I just have to keep dreaming and doing my thing, trying to make something that everyone can enjoy.

EIGHT WAYS TO MAKE EVERYTHING AWESOME

1. Add candy

2. Lots of whipped cream

3. Involve sports in it

4. Remember your phone charger

5. Wear new sneakers

6. Invite your friends

7. Great food

8. Make a game of it

My First Girlfriend

**Maybe it's love but I'm not really sure.
Either way, I gotta step it up and act mature.**

I think love is something God puts inside us. Even before we can talk, we end up being able to show it in different ways. Our first loves are Mom and Dad. They're the ones we see and cling to and need.

Then love begins to grow up, as we do. The love we have for our brothers and sisters and everyone in our families. Next is for our friends and classmates and teachers. Last is for those people we don't even know yet.

How old do we have to be before we can truly understand the word "love"? I don't think we'll ever fully understand it, but I think as each year passes, we learn more about it.

So can a fourth-grader sing about being in love with a girl? I think so—even though we have been careful about doing this. But by the fourth grade, you can have a crush for sure. Sometimes you can even call yourself "boyfriend and girlfriend."

What do *those* words mean, exactly? A lot of different things! It really depends on who's saying them. Mars had a girlfriend named Rebecca, who we all loved. He sure loved her, too, because they've since gotten engaged and married.

So "boyfriend and girlfriend" can mean "future marriage," but not always.

I remember a girlfriend I had when I was in the fourth grade. She was a friend, and she was definitely a girl! The summer after fourth grade, we went to the beach for a baseball tournament. I would never have imagined that this is where I would have my first experience with really thinking about love for someone other than my family. Sure, I had thought some girls were cute, but never enough to want to do something about it. Until that one day.

We were all having fun at the beach and hanging out with friends, and I looked up at this one girl I had known for a while. I don't really know what happened, but she suddenly looked different. I guess you could say it was "puppy love." Why do they call it that, anyway?

After a while, I got the nerve to ask my parents if I could have a girlfriend. They said no, because they thought I was too young. I can be pretty persistent and convincing, though. Finally, after lecturing me and quizzing me a bit on what that phrase meant to me, they said okay. They gave in with one condition. I had to ask the girl's mom for her permission. I think my parents assumed I would chicken out and never talk to another parent about this.

I have to admit, it did take me a little time to get up the nerve. But finally, I did do it. Talk about being nervous! I could not believe I was actually asking her mom if I could "date" her daughter. Whatever "date" actually meant. I did not really know, but it sounded good and I knew it was something Mars had done with Becca.

Her mom smiled at me and said yes.

She said yes!

Remember Rudolph in the Christmas movie when the girl reindeer said Rudolph could walk her home after school? He jumped through the air saying, "She said yes, she said yes!" I know just how he felt. When her mom told me that, I felt like I could fly, too.

But now I had to do something else. Now I had to ask the girl herself if *she* wanted to date me. I thought she liked me the same way I liked her, but I really didn't know for sure. We had only been friends.

This is like being on a roller coaster, I remember thinking.

Your stomach just goes crazy with the excitement and fear all at the same time. You ask yourself, *What am I doing? What have I gotten myself into?* But when I actually got the nerve to ask, guess what? She said *yes!* What an awesome day. It's one I don't think I'll ever forget. At least, I hope not.

That was a great summer and continued on through the next school year. So, yeah . . . my first girlfriend.

Eventually, it started to seem harder. We never had problems at all. She was the best, and our friendship never changed. But with both of us in different schools and in lots of extra activities, it became less of a priority for us, so we decided to just be friends. I am not sure what we were looking for, but it was definitely not the time to follow in Mars's and Becca's footsteps at our age.

Looking back, was it silly?

I don't think so.

Other guys can make fun of you for liking a girl, and it's too easy to just brush it off and act cool. To be like, *Emotions are for girls and I'm all about being tough and cool.* The truth is, only young boys would think that. Grown men like Mars and my dad don't feel that way at all. They're married, sure, but they're still girlfriend and boyfriend with their wives. They're still friends with them, and it shows.

Don't Be Afraid to Look Stupid

People are gonna talk about whatever you do, so you might as well go for it and just be the best YOU.

I f you have a talent, don't be afraid to show it. Even if those voices inside you tell you not to.

But what if I think I can sing but really can't?

Do you love to sing? Then sing. You can always get better. Do it because you love to do it.

But what if my dance moves really look ridiculous?

So what? Be yourself. I'm sure I've had some dance moves that have looked silly. I just laugh and keep trying.

I'm afraid I'll let the team down.

It's called a team because all of you have to do this thing together. If I'm playing basketball or football, sometimes I stink it up. Sometimes we just don't play our best. But keep at it, and don't let your frustrations shut you down.

I wrote a song, but it's too personal to share.

But didn't you write it because you wanted to share it? You could start by showing it to someone you trust and who cares about you.

I've never really tried this before.

There has never been a better time to try it than *now*.

I might look stupid.

We all look stupid from time to time, so just do it and don't worry if others laugh. Your friends get you. If you go for it, they'll understand.

Have fun, try things out, be vulnerable, and put yourself out there.

The only bad thing is holding back because you're afraid.

The more things you try and the more you put yourself out there, the easier it becomes, every single time!

Touring

**You never know where you'll go,
when you're on the road doing shows**

In 2013, at the age of ten, my musical career really began to take off. I'd end up doing six concerts from June to December that year, with another dozen coming in both 2014 and 2015.

They say practice makes perfect, right?

That's a lie, because nothing's ever perfect. But we certainly did get better with each show. I performed at places like Six Flags in Saint Louis and House of Blues in Dallas. I'd have another New York City concert at The Town Hall and one in Anaheim, California, at the City National Grove.

A lot of young girls would come up to me and look a bit like they were lost. Unsure and not saying a word, even when I thanked them for coming and gave them a flower. Then there'd be the groups. The girls in groups were the exact opposite. Four girls would sound like forty, jumping up and down and screaming my name.

I'd continue to rehearse the moves and memorize my lines. In addition to my regular school homework, I had musical homework, too. Before each show, I'd sit backstage listening to the lyrics on my headphones and making sure I'd get them right.

Of course, I might also be doing something like wrestling with my brothers. We might warm up by arm wrestling or body slamming, and as long as no one broke a bone or got a bloody nose, it was fine.

The concerts would also be a chance to collaborate with other musicians and dancers. I'd have different artists join me on the tour, like the Haschak Sisters, JoJo Siwa, Chanel Lóran, Brooke and Carissa Adee, and many others. It's been fun, because I've done videos with a lot of these singers, so it was a chance to perform with them and also give them exposure to the BBoys and BGirls.

Seizing the Moment

You wanna do it? I'll tell you what it's about.
Seizing the moment
and deciding to go all out!

emember how I told you the story about me going down to Mars in the basement of our house and telling him I wanted him to film me recording a rap? Crazy to think that in just three years, it would become touring and releasing songs and having T-shirts and posters ("merch," as it's called in the business).

It would keep growing, too.

My father and Mars taught me something at a very young age: seize the moment.

Mars could have ignored the moment and kept trying to build the fan base for MarsRaps. Yet he decided it was the right time to jump on what was happening with MattyBRaps. So did my parents.

I was just having fun jumping around to the songs. I didn't understand anything about seizing any kind of moment. But the older I become, the more I realize what that looks like. I also know that you don't have to be on the verge of becoming a pop musician in order to seize a moment. Every day we're presented with a bunch of opportunities to do something meaningful. A situation is there, and we're able to choose to be brave and bold and to believe in something—or else to simply do nothing.

You could stick up for someone being picked on or bullied.

You could stand firm when somebody wants to make a bad decision.

You could refuse to give up and continue to work hard—as hard as you ever have in your whole life.

You could be telling the truth, when a lie would be easier.

Seizing the moment doesn't just have to be about something massive. Each day, it's the small moments that count. All anyone ever has is "right now," and you have a choice about what you are going to do with it.

Be on the lookout for opportunities, and when they do come, seize them!

You never know, people. You never know.

Back in Time

I got a futuristic flow and a futuristic mind, but I'll stop for a moment and take you all back in time.

Making my song and video for "Back in Time" was a blast. We worked with the people putting out the animated movie *Free Birds*, and I was able to film it with my first dance crew (Lil Dee Dee, Elijah, Hannah, and Emily), which I called "The Posse." I was excited that they would be part of this original song, which would be featured on the movie soundtrack. This was an awesome film about two turkeys from opposite sides of the tracks traveling back in time to change history. So for our video, we did something similar and had me going back in time in order to save music.

The music video included throwbacks to some styles of music videos from Michael Jackson, NSYNC, and Vanilla Ice. I even got to dance and sing with the main animated bird character from the movie in my video.

If I could really go back in time, what are some places I'd love to visit? That's a hard question.

My first thought is to imagine what it was like for those who actually met Jesus in person and what it was like to ask him questions.

176

I'd love to see Moses parting the Red Sea and Jonah being swallowed by the whale. I don't need to see those things in order to have faith that they happened, but I do think they'd be cool to see. A whale swallowing a man whole? Come on!

I think of historic events and sporting events and things like going back to see what my mother and father were like in sixth grade. But I'll stick to music, because that's my world.

So here are five artists I would have loved to see live, if I had a time machine and a magic ticket dispenser.

1. Elvis Presley's first concert on July 30, 1954. Elvis was nineteen years old when he performed his first concert at the Overton Park Orchestra Shell in Memphis, Tennessee. It'd be awesome to see him performing for the first time.

2. The Beatles' last performance together on a rooftop in London in 1969.

3. Michael Jackson on the *Bad* tour in 1987. It was one of his best albums, and the tour was said to be Jackson in his prime.

4. MC Hammer during his "U Can't Touch This" and "2 Legit 2 Quit" era in 1990–91. I'd love to see him busting moves on the stage in those awesome Hammer pants.

5. Outkast in 2003 (the year I was born). This was the year their big album *Speakerboxxx/The Love Below* came out. I'd

love to see "Hey Ya" in concert the first time it was performed.

There are lots and lots of artists I'd love to see now, not just because I love their music, but to see and study how they do things. Hopefully, the older I get, the more concerts and live events I'll be able to attend.

Santa's Been Good to Me

You know **I'm unrehearsed,** but I'm safety first!

Work hard, play hard. That's a motto for a lot of people, including myself.

At the age of ten, I'd started really getting into Airsoft. If you've never played this or heard of it, Airsoft is a game where you get gear and Airsoft guns and attempt to hit your opponents. The guns shoot pellets, so while it's not dangerous if you wear your safety gear, you still have to be careful and always wear your helmet and facemask to protect your eyes.

The key is managing to shoot the other players while not getting hit. If you are hit, you have to man up and take yourself out of the game—even if no one else saw it. There are indoor and outdoor courses that you can play, with lots of people or even just a handful of your friends.

I remember one time early on. After doing some recording, Mars and I and some other guys went to play Airsoft for about four hours. It was incredible. At the end, I left with marks all over my legs and knuckles, but it was so much fun.

One great thing about having an online presence was getting to share my passion for playing Airsoft with the fans. I guess the Airsoft GI company noticed, because they surprised me on Christmas 2013 with a bunch of Airsoft guns.

Like . . . a bunch!

I got a full metal M-4 rifle.

I also got a SCAR-H rifle that came with a scope, laser pointer, and a suppressor.

They also sent me things like a mask and goggles and a vest and a gun bag.

How awesome is that?

Oh, and I can't forget the *massive* sniper rifle, complete with a scope and a tripod.

I'm gonna be unbeatable in Airsoft!

I couldn't believe that having videos with lots of views meant that suddenly an awesome company like Airsoft was giving me gifts! I didn't promote them with any reward in mind, I just wanted to talk about it in my videos! All because I'm a big fan.

So if you've never played it before, check out Airsoft.

And always—always—follow these rules:

1. Always wear something to protect your face and eyes while playing.

2. Only play at official fields.

3. Always transport your Airsoft guns in a gun bag.

4. Keep your finger off the trigger all the time unless shooting.

Good luck and good hunting!

Light of the World

**I want to shine bright for the world to see.
And I hope You are smiling down on me.**

Christmas is such a great time of the year. We get a couple of weeks off from school, our family gets together to eat and exchange gifts. There is lots and lots of food to enjoy. We get awesome presents. It really is one of the best times out of the whole year.

Obviously, Christmas is a lot more than just those things. All of those things are a result of the reason we're celebrating. It's not really about Santa, it's about that baby in the manger named Jesus Christ.

That's why my family celebrates Christmas, and why it's so important to us.

There's this really cool thing I read about called the Advent wreath. Around this wreath are four candles with another candle in the center. Each week, a candle is lit on the wreath to represent one thing, then the final one is lit on Christmas Day.

The meanings behind each candle are really special, so I thought I'd share them with you.

The first candle represents hope. It's a reminder that we need to put our hopes in God and he will bless them.

The second candle is for faith. This means that we need to remember what Christmas is all about—Christ being born and what he stands for.

The third candle stands for joy. This is what we're supposed to feel about Christmas, not just with all the festivities, but being joyful about the fact that Christ was born on this day.

The fourth candle stands for peace. What a nice candle to light in these holy days.

Finally, the large candle in the middle is lit on Christmas day. This is to stand for Jesus being the light and savior of the world.

I've talked a lot about trying to be a spark and a light in this world and someone who gets to spread hope and joy out there. The only way I'm truly able to do it is because of this light that I believe in—the kind that shines not only at Christmastime, but all year long.

If I can share a tiny bit of that light through these songs and videos, then that's everything to me.

Part Five

I'M STILL IN MIDDLE SCHOOL SO . . . I THINK THAT WE SHOULD JUST BE FRIENDS

Turned Out the Lights

Always **believe in yourself** and dream,
even if there are **words that sting.**

Bullying is a big deal these days, and there are so many ways it can happen. It's not just in the hallways or classrooms of a school. It can take place online. It can happen with messaging and texting, with tweeting or commenting online, and on social media. It has never been easier to put people down.

At the start of 2014, we made a special song and video to highlight the difficult circumstances some people go through and to encourage an environment of love and respect at school and home. "Turned Out the Lights" featured Maddi Jane, and it has a truly great message.

I've received lots of notes from fans who've shared how my music has helped them through tough periods in their lives. We wanted to illustrate these struggles and encourage others to think before criticizing or laughing at another person.

Mars said he was proud of me for wanting to address some of the issues we tackled in the video. It's not just about abuse or bullying, but it also talks about things like peer pressure and verbal abuse from parents at home. While my home life is the best a kid could hope for, I am bullied online all the time. I've always continued to try to sing and rap about things that relate to me, so this issue was something that was definitely meaningful and personally relevant.

I'm a kid full of hopes and dreams, and I've always been telling people to keep doing the same. But it's not easy for everybody.

I've been surrounded by lots of prayer and praise and I'm so grateful for that. But not everybody has these forms of support.

Sometimes it's hard to achieve when you can't believe.

This could be anybody talking, any kid out there who's feeling this way. I wanted to show that they're important and also understood. That there's still hope for them.

We filmed the video at The Atlanta Academy. They were awesome to allow us to come in and film in their classrooms. Their goal was the same as ours: to help promote an environment for children to grow with love and respect from everyone, from students to faculty.

We used The Actor's Scene in Atlanta to cast the roles in the video. One kid named Ryan played the part of the person being bullied.

"What was special about this was that I was a part of making a difference in someone's life," Ryan said. "And letting them know there is always a way."

Hal Whiteside, the actor playing the abusive father in the video, summed up our goal with this cool project. "One song or one video can change a kid's outlook and perspective on their situation."

That's what I keep trying to do with every new song.

What a Birthday Party Should and Shouldn't Be

When life starts moving at a faster pace, don't forget to celebrate!

Ever go to a friend's birthday party and end up leaving feeling a bit . . . bored, maybe? Or maybe even bothered by the fact that the whole party was all about the birthday boy or girl? Maybe sad or mad about some of the stuff that happened?

I'm all about parties and celebrating another year of turning older. But here are the things I think birthday parties should avoid.

Invite Groups, Not Just Friends

Of course you should invite your friends, but make sure you think about all the kids in your life. Let's say you have a class with only five other girls in it, and you're only really close with four of them. Do I have to even say the obvious? No. What if you invite only half of the guys on the football team? Or only half the kids in the neighborhood you play with? *Don't do it.*

Sometimes you have to keep the numbers low, but still think in terms of groups. *Just my classmates. Just my four closest buds. How about everyone I know, expecting half of them not to come?*

Don't Make It All about You

Obviously, a birthday is a chance to say, "Hey, world, look at me, I'm a year older!" It's the day people are going to say nice things about you, or at the very least say "happy birthday," even if it's only online somewhere. A spotlight's going to be on you, whatever you do, so don't *overdo* things.

Are you having a birthday party? Think of the timing, and make it fall on a date that works out best for your friends (and their parents). Send out invites with enough notice. Don't make a big deal about presents. Maybe you don't want anybody to even bring presents. Or better yet, maybe everybody can donate something to a cause or charity.

Think of games and things to do that include everybody. Try not to have it resemble the schoolyard, where cliques all gather together.

When deciding on the food, think of others as well. Maybe *you* really do love anchovies, but does that mean you should get it on the whole pizza? If one of your classmates can't eat wheat, does he get something instead of cake?

Get a little party favor for everybody coming. It doesn't have to be expensive—it's just a simple way to say "thank you for showing up." These kids are coming to the party because of you, so show that you appreciate them.

Be Creative

I'm not talking about trying to get One Direction to play at your birthday party. Creative doesn't mean spending lots of money or doing anything too crazy. Here are some random and fun ideas:

- ✦ **Make something.** Maybe you'll be creating pizzas that you end up eating. Or maybe all of you can make individual desserts. Decorating cupcakes or cookies with icing and candies and sprinkles. Would this be messy? Yeah. Would it also be fun? Absolutely!

- ✦ **Organize an activity.** Maybe get everybody to write an original rap (of course I'd suggest that). Give everybody a piece of paper and a number of lines to write, then everybody has to put it together. You could have a rap battle at the end and declare a winner.

- ✦ **Play games.** Put people on teams who never talk or hang out together. Have them play a sport or a board game. Maybe it's charades or challenges or other team games. What starts off as a team could end up as a friendship.

Don't Force It

You might have a great and creative idea that ends up flopping. Maybe you paired Susie and Amy on a team to play Would You Rather, and suddenly they're fighting. Feel free to switch gears and do something different. Always have a plan B, in case plan A starts to blow up.

Parents Are on Your Side

Involve your parents beyond just having them pay for the food and decorations and so on. Let's say you're going to a roller-skating party and some of your friends don't know how to skate. Get your mom or dad to show them some pointers, which they probably did for you when you first learned. Parents can also help break up cliques or clashes, and they can always change the gears of the party if and when necessary.

Don't Ignore Siblings

It's the worst when your sibling has a party at your house and then doesn't include you in any way. Not that I'm speaking from personal experience . . . *Or am I?*

I do know that someone like Sarah Grace doesn't give anyone the option of excluding her. When she wants to be involved, she's involved. But not all younger brothers and sisters are as assertive and crafty as Sarah Grace.

Involve your younger siblings!

Think of them as the party mascots. Maybe they can't do everything the older kids are doing, but they can still be a part of the event in some way. Your friends might not even know your little brother or sister that well, so this is their chance. Don't make your parents get involved and *force* you to do this.

Appreciate the Moment

Your friends are all around you. You're doing something fun and laughing lots. You'll probably be eating something really sweet and not so good for you very soon. Then you might be opening some presents.

How awesome is this?

Don't take it for granted. Think of how lucky you are to have a party like this. Seek out ways to encourage your friends. Be kind. Compliment them. Show appreciation. Be silly, but don't steal the show.

It's your birthday, so you deserve to enjoy it—and so do your guests!

Listen and Learn

Wanna be the fastest?
You'll play like you practice.

In order to become better at anything, there are two things you need to do.

The first thing is obvious. You have to practice.

The actor and singer Will Smith said this about practicing: "I've always considered myself to be just average talent and what I have is a ridiculous insane obsessiveness for practice and preparation."

I'm not sure I'd call Will Smith an "average talent," but I do think his practice and preparation show up in everything he does. Practicing means doing something over and over and over again. Even if you love this thing, you might end up really getting tired of doing it. But you have to keep going, because that's how you get better.

The more music I made, the more opportunities I had to perform it. This naturally meant needing to practice more. I ended up practicing downstairs in our basement in the room where we watch the big-screen television. It's big enough to allow me to perform as if I'm onstage.

Whenever I practiced for an upcoming show, I'd get the microphone and plug it in and then would perform a set for Mom, Dad, Mars, and usually Sarah Grace. They could listen and give me tips and suggestions. It always helped to do this in front of them.

This brings me to the other thing you need in order to get better at something, which is to be critiqued continually. You need people to let you know how you're doing, and they need to be honest and tell you everything. Some people call it constructive criticism, and many of us hate to hear it. Sometimes words can be unkind and not helpful in the least, but getting advice and input from someone who cares about you only helps.

You don't always have to take their advice, but if they're older than you, that usually means they're wiser, too. Be willing to listen and learn. Realize that nobody is perfect, and all you can do is keep trying to get better.

I have to sing that note in tune. I have to say that phrase correctly. I have to remember the dance steps. I have to finish the song strong.

My parents and Mars will pick out these little things here and there that I need to do, but I always know they're there to help me out. Sometimes I don't want to hear it at first.

"I'm trying my best!" I might say.

But then I remember that when I keep practicing, my best keeps getting better.

Change

You're not always **dealt the upper hand.**
Sometimes you **gotta change plans.**

Have you ever had a great idea and planned something out, only to see it totally backfire? Suddenly everything changes and goes out of your control? Not all things will go your way, so you have to be willing to deal with change and go with the flow.

A small example of this happened when Mars and I were shooting the video for my version of One Republic's "Counting Stars." I fell in love with the song, since it's about one of the things I love most in life: following your dreams. We planned an outdoor shoot at the Chattapoochee Dog Park that was near the Chattahoochee River.

Well, that's what we had *planned.* Suddenly we found ourselves in a downpour. We tried to wait it out in the car, which allowed me to get some homework done (since I have to do homework like every other kid in the country!). The rain just kept coming, so we had to call it a day.

But . . .

We still had the evening to work everything out. We just had to shift gears. In this case, we were able to finish the video with some shots outside on the deck of my house. In the end, we had a video that was actually cooler than the original concept we'd been planning on.

That was a great lesson—sometimes a change can happen that leads to bigger and better things.

Maybe there's something in your life, like outdoor plans that have to change because of the weather. Maybe it's something major like a parent changing jobs and you have to move across the country. Some things in life are out of your control, but they're never out of God's control. Trust that things will work out. Believe that change can actually lead to better things in your life. They really can. You just have to keep positive, have faith, and keep pursuing great things for yourself.

Before Every Show

Pray without ceasing.

1 Thessalonians 5:17

It's always a crazy time before each concert, since there are so many things going on. Sometimes there will be fans to meet or something to record or just needing to make sure everything for the concert is set up.

However busy it might be, it's never too busy to stop and pray before we go onstage.

It's something we always do.

We pray that all of us performing can shine bright for God. We ask that God can share our light with whoever might be watching, both that night and in the future.

We ask for safety for everybody involved, not just those of us performing but everybody in the venue.

We ask God to help us all remember our lyrics and the choreography and all the things we need to remember during the performance.

We pray for the lights and the sound and the equipment to all work properly.

We also ask God to bless every single person who's coming to watch us. We pray that they'll have a great experience and be able to return home safely.

The shows are a lot of work, but they're also a lot of fun. They're busy with lots of people involved.

Whatever you're doing, stop and ask God for his strength and his guidance. You can never pray too much!

My Atlanta Peeps

**An incredible night and I'll spend it with you
I'm in Atlanta living life
like a dream come true.**

Thank you, Atlanta.

Thank you for coming out to the Georgia World Congress Center on January 25, 2014.

Thanks to all eighteen hundred–plus of you. All my BBoys and BGirls showing up and standing and singing and dancing with me.

More than eighteen hundred people. That's crazy and awesome.

I love to see the BGirls and BBoys who were able to come backstage and say hi. Seeing their surprise and their smiles always makes this so incredible.

Then to see everybody out there having fun and enjoying the night.

It's intense and unreal.

Thanks to all of you who join me as I perform for over an hour.

It's nights like this that make me want to keep singing and dancing and performing and playing.

I'm going to keep this up.

I feel natural up there rapping and sharing my songs with all of you.

I'm so grateful for your beautiful smiles.

Four years with all of you? It's all gone by so fast, and it's been a blast.

Thank you, Atlanta. The home of BNation.

NINE FAVORITE FOODS
(IN NO PARTICULAR ORDER):

✦ **Cool Whip**

✦ **Pizza**

✦ **Grilled cheese**

✦ **Mac and cheese**

✦ **Sour Patch Kids**

✦ **Reese's Peanut Butter Cups**

✦ **Avocados**

✦ **Jolly Ranchers**

✦ **Frozen drinks (Frappuccinos, Blizzards, milkshakes)**

Black and Blue

Focus on your journey and keep climbing.
Every time it rains, just find that silver lining.

Perhaps you're heading outside to look up at the stars, but you end up only getting rained on. What should you do?

Make the most of the moment. It's not like those stars are suddenly gone, right? They're still there.

Don't let some clouds cover the lights.

Don't let some storms crash over your dreams.

Maybe the day began with something breaking.

Maybe your best friend just said something mean to you.

Maybe something you worked hard on didn't end up being so great.

Maybe you just don't feel so special today.

Maybe everybody else in your life is more successful than you.

Maybe your team lost.

Maybe your report got an F.

Maybe you just got your heart torn apart.

Maybe that blue sky you're looking at feels gray because of your mood.

If any of those moments occur during the day, close your eyes and pray.

Believe that today can be a good day.

Try to make up your mind that things can be not only okay, but they can be awesome!

Tell yourself to stand up and stand strong.

Remember that broken things can be fixed.

Remember that friends—even best friends—can make mistakes and should be forgiven.

Remember that it takes a lot of work to do great things, and all you can do is to keep doing.

Remember that you are special every single day.

Remember that we're all different, but that's what makes us all incredible.

Remember that someone always has to lose when competing, but it's not about winning or losing.

Remember that after a failure, you can only go *up*.

Remember that love always protects, always trusts, always hopes, always perseveres.

And always remember that behind every sky, whether it's clear blue or black clouds, God is watching and loving you.

Simple

From old songs to new songs, my oh my. Sometimes the best thing is to simplify.

If you've ever seen my vlog showing off the place we make and record my music, you'll see that it's pretty simple. It's a soundproof room in our basement where we watch television that's perfect for playing music and even rehearsing. The room next to it is smaller and consists of a desk and workstation, a couch and table, and the place my microphone is set up.

This is where it all happens.

Mars likes to say the instrument he plays is the computer, and it's true. We'll record, and then he'll begin making the magic happen on the iMac.

There aren't lots of machines or mics we use. There aren't lots of different gadgets or expensive tools. Mars has been using the same camera from the very beginning to record all the videos we've done.

Sometimes people worry a lot about all those other things. The right equipment and software and a great-looking studio to record in, and on and on. We try to just worry about what's inside our hearts and souls.

Simple can be the perfect solution. Don't let anybody else fool you into thinking otherwise.

Lifeguarding Eleven

Sitting by the pool, just trying to play it cool.

At eleven, my fantasy job was lifeguard.

How cool would that be?

It's not because I'd be sitting all day. The lifeguards I see are usually walking around the pool or water park making sure everything's okay.

It's not because I'd be around pretty girls all day.

Well, okay, maybe that is *one* reason.

But the main thing is I'd be able to train in rescuing people. Helping them get out of the water and performing CPR and doing all the necessary things. I'm sure I'd also become a much better swimmer. Water parks and swimming pools are fun places. They're getaways for families. They're full of fun.

After my shift, I could give a performance for everybody at the pool. I could perform "Summer" by Calvin Harris or "Summertime" by DJ Jazzy Jeff and the Fresh Prince. Or I could go really far back and do my version of "Surfin' Safari" by the Beach Boys. I'd have a nice tan and make some new friends. Yeah. So if I realized all this by eleven, why didn't I pull it off by age twelve?

Maybe I will get a chance when I'm thirteen . . .

True Colors, Part I

I'll love you forever, and **always** you'll be
somebody **who means** a lot to me.

Hey, Mars."

"Yeah, Matt?"

"Let's go big."

"What's that?"

"With our next video, let's go big or go home."

"Well, technically we *are* home, Matt."

"I'm talking about reaching people. We need a big video."

"So what do you mean by 'big'?"

"We need something that will be viewed by fifty million people."

"Is that all?"

"Maybe even more."

"Okay, Matt—well, what do you want the video to be about?"

"Sarah Grace."

"Let's do it."

Chyeah . . .

Okay, so that's not how the idea for my rendition of "True Colors" went. It would have been cool. I'm talking to Mars and I'm all like, "Yo, Mars, we need fifty million views" and he's like, "Yo, man, let's do it," and Sarah Grace is like, "Yo, I need to be a part of this," and then we're all like, "What's up with all these yo's?"

There was no grand plan for any number of views. We just did what felt right at the moment. It was indeed time to shine a light on Sarah Grace, who many of the fans already knew. They'd had a glimpse of Sarah Grace and wanted more. The awesome thing was that Sarah Grace wanted more, too.

It was time.

Time to launch a rainbow over the roof of the world, courtesy of my very talented and beautiful sister.

True Colors, Part 2

You're different to the world,
but you're beautiful to me.
I'm so proud of who you want to be.

The song and the video are very near and dear to our hearts. With each passing song and video, Sarah Grace has continued to love being at my side and stealing the spotlight. She's a natural onstage and behind the scenes. It's so obvious when you see it. And people have really enjoyed watching the videos when the two of us are in them.

Sarah Grace kept telling us how much she loved acting and how she wanted to be in a video. She had made her debut in our version of "Just the Way You Are" by Bruno Mars. People loved it. So now my parents decided it was the right time to give Sarah Grace her own platform.

Fans had already been asking for Sarah Grace to have her own YouTube channel.

Some might think that was strange. Giving a young girl with Down syndrome her own YouTube channel?

But this was how the Sarah Grace Club was born. It was another way to shine some light in the world and to encourage and inspire all those affected by family members and friends with Down syndrome. To share what it's about and to show people who don't understand it that someone like Sarah Grace is unique and gifted, just like so many others.

Sarah Grace just wants to show love and joy and make people smile.

Our version of Cyndi Lauper's "True Colors" was a way to spread the news about dealing with people with differences. The video isn't just about people with Down syndrome. Sarah Grace stood for anybody who feels different.

Maybe people with differences among them—whether it's race or gender or culture or different abilities—can connect with each other in ways no others can. Maybe we can learn and grow from each other. Maybe we can see God's love in a different way, just like the way we've been able to see it with Sarah Grace.

Sarah Grace really has captured the hearts and minds of so many people. Who knows? Maybe she'll be writing her own book one day.

True Colors, Part 3

There's always room for change.

All the time, I see people putting others down for their differences.

It's so easy for one group to make fun of another, to cut down the center and divide. All for what? For someone being different? We're all different.

What does true beauty really mean? To me, true beauty is watching Sarah Grace in the video for "True Colors."

Sarah Grace was quite the actress when we recorded it. My little sister was amazing. She was no longer that little girl just walking around the garden being adorable. Nope—she was acting and playing a part.

Who hasn't ever felt like the outcast, alone, left out?

It's so easy to focus on yourself and not focus on the needs of others.

Sometimes it's easy to judge others for circumstances they have no control over.

Maybe there is something about them that is different from the other kids you know.

Those differences might even seem funny at the time, but making fun of someone is not what being a leader is all about.

Being big and standing strong can mean making hard decisions.

Like in the video when the girl rings the doorbell to reach out. She put herself out there. She didn't know how she would be received. Would the door go unanswered, or even get slammed in her face?

Of course, with Sarah Grace, the girl is going to get pulled into the house to play.

It's always easier to be the same as everyone else, instead of being different. But it's true that we are all equal, and love conquers all.

Sarah Grace has shown us that love since the moment she was born. What an incredible gift she has, to be able to share that love with the rest of the world.

TEN WAYS I PREPARE AND GET PUMPED UP

THIS INCLUDES GETTING READY FOR A SHOW AND PLAYING SPORTS.

1. Listen to music with a sick beat

2. Dance

3. Relax by playing games on my phone

4. Throw a ball around backstage

5. Eat some candy

6. Listen to more hyped-up music

7. Stretch

8. Visualize the moment and the fans

9. Stay hydrated

10. Pray

Reworking

You want everything you touch to be an instant success, but sometimes a "do-over" is part of the process.

There have been lots of songs that I'll end up discovering or hearing that I think, *Hey, I could flip that into a MattyB rap.* But a lot of times, the songs are too adult or too edgy or . . . too something. When the song is "too something," it usually means I can't do it. But occasionally, I'll be able to figure out a way around this. "Drop Dirty" is one of those. Our parody flipped the lyrics from Jason Derulo's song "Talk Dirty," which was obviously inappropriate for us, and instead made it about dropping a beat.

This doesn't work for all songs. I mean, Mars and I are creative, but we can't perform miracles. Sometimes I'll try something and there will be no way. My dad will just look at me and shake his head. Ideas themselves are never bad, unless you decide to run with the bad ones. That's where judgment comes in. Mars and I get together and brainstorm different ideas, then my father weighs in. He tells us to have a clear vision before making a song and a video.

For the "Drop Dirty" video, we collaborated with Chloe Channell. She got to see how Team MattyB does things—from recording and singing to the craziness of a video shoot. The most fun thing about doing songs like this has been meeting people and having a good time.

Get Out There and Go for It

Don't let life just pass you by.
Get out there and do it, it doesn't hurt to try.

When I was ten, I really wanted to start playing lacrosse. John Michael, Josh, and I had always played baseball. I also had my music career that I was working on, plus voice lessons and dance lessons and tumbling. I didn't really know much about lacrosse, except what my neighbors were teaching me. They gave me an old stick to practice with. Josh wanted to try his hand at it, too.

We knew that we couldn't play lacrosse in the spring, because it would interfere with baseball. But then we had an idea, which we shared with our parents.

"They have an indoor winter league for lacrosse," I told Dad. "You go every weekend, and it's for seven weekends, and you play one game each time." It's called "box lacrosse."

Dad was skeptical, saying we didn't know how to play and that it might mess us up in baseball. Even if we liked it, we still couldn't play in the regular season, because of baseball. I think he was afraid we would like it and then we would beg to change over to playing lacrosse, after investing years in baseball lessons and practices. Mom didn't even believe that we knew how to play lacrosse, but Josh and I kept on them. Finally, we convinced them to let us try it.

We both had a great time on our box lacrosse teams. Josh did go back to baseball in the spring, but I had lacrosse fever. Yep—Dad's fear had to come to pass. I would have to convince him that those baseball lessons and practices were not lost, but would now serve me well in lacrosse. I could *not* put the stick down—you could say I was obsessed. Fortunately for me, our travel baseball team had split up anyway, and it was the perfect time to try something new for the spring.

Our spring lacrosse team would end up going undefeated, and would play in the championship game. We lost that championship by one goal. That was a sad day, but what a great season we had. It was a season to be proud of, and it was one that locked me into this new sport.

I was glad I'd gone out there and tried new things, even if I had to overcome some doubts. I decided to go out there and give it my best, and it really paid off.

Three Main Elements to Each Show

I wanna see a smile on your face when you leave this place.

We put a lot of work and creativity and thought into each one of my shows. If I were to name the three main elements to the show, they'd be the following:

1. **Include a female vocalist.** Each of my shows has a vocalist who will sing between my sets. This allows me to take a quick break, change, and get prepared for the next set. It's also a nice change of pace for the audience, and the crowd always seems to enjoy it.

2. **Some great choreography.** We always try to add new things and make the moves really strong. We think of how we move around each other, plus how we can work together with the song and the images on the screen behind us.

3. **There's the rapping, singing, and performing itself.** I put everything I can into each song. The dancers around

me are bringing it. You gotta make something your own, beyond the basic choreography.

I have had some awesome dancers who have become great friends, as well. We make sure to have fun, because it'll show through when we're onstage. Hopefully, we'll be in front of you soon, putting on one of the greatest shows you've ever seen.

It Is What It Is

Sometimes it rains.

Sometimes it pours.

Ever read the book *Alexander and the Terrible, Horrible, No Good, Very Bad Day* by Judith Viorst? It's about a kid who has the worst day of his life, with lots and lots of bad things happening to him.

I think all of us can relate from time to time.

Like one show I can remember—it seemed like nothing went right. One of our dancers got sick. Then we couldn't remember some of the choreography for one of the songs. We were trying to figure it out. This was just one hour before the show was going to start!

At the merch table, my most popular T-shirt didn't arrive with the other merchandise. They spent a while looking for the shipment, but nobody could find it.

One of the outfits for the dancers ended up not exactly fitting right, so Mom and the others had to scramble to get something else ready in time.

Even when things do go right, the day of any show is a bit crazy. People are running around, dealing with different things.

As Mom and Dad tell me, you can't get upset.

"It is what it is," Dad will say.

The key is always to stay calm and to come up with solutions. Why waste energy on being frustrated when you can spend it on trying to fix the problem? For us, we have to remember something: this isn't about us. It's not about how Matt or Mars or Mom or Dad feel. It's about making sure the fans have the best possible time they can have.

This is a good example of how we should take every day that comes at us. Each day, there's going to be something that ends up going wrong. People can let us down. Plans can change. Things can break, whether it's a car or a phone or even someone's heart.

When these things happen, should we tell ourselves *I hate life and nothing good ever happens to me?*

I sure hope that's not the response! Try to remember what my dad said: *it is what it is.*

This thing happened. Okay. Now what?

Let's say you're on a boat with friends, and your phone slips out of your hand and sinks to the bottom of the lake. All right. First things first—you probably need to call your parents and tell them what happened. Um, wait—no. First, you need to borrow someone else's phone.

No amount of anger is going to get that phone back, right? Find solutions to the problem. If there aren't any, accept it and move on.

We all have things happen to us. The only part we control is how we respond.

Collaborating

I mic check with the **ones and twos.**
Only thing this song needs is a **feature** from you.

No matter what age you are, if you're a human being, you will have to learn to work with others. When you're the youngest of four brothers, you learn at a very early age. Maybe even at birth!

Everything in life is a collaboration, whether it's being part of a class or on a team or being in a family or filming a video. You have to be willing to share ideas and be open to hearing people out.

With each passing year, I've found myself working with lots of different people. It has been exciting to meet lots of talented singers, dancers, actors, and even celebrities who I've done videos with.

First, let me list some of the singers who have recorded with me:

Julia Sheer

Meghan Tonjes

Cimorelli sisters

Madilyn Bailey

Jack Vidgen

Alex G

Tyler Ward

Jason Chen

Athena Skye

Maddi Jane

James Maslow

Skylar Stecker

Carlos Guevara

Nyielle

Coco Jones

Lil Will Robertson

Chloe Channell

Carissa Adee

Brooke Adee

Olivia Kay

Jordyn Jones

John-Robert Rimel

Ivey Meeks

Chanel Lóran

Haschak Sisters

Ricky Garcia

Darby Cappillino

And of course, my big cousin Marshall Manning!

Wow . . . listing those names reminds me of all the amazing and talented people I've been able to meet and work with—and that's just some of them! Shout-out and thanks to everyone who has ever been a part of a MattyB video. In addition to singers, I have had the privilege to work with my close homies (or posse) who have acted or danced in my videos, like Carson, Druw, Jack, Kate, Liv, Justin, Jake, and dancers Madison, Gracie, Sierra, Olivia, Jojo, Laneya Grace, Kalliyan, Lil DeeDee, Elijah, Hannah, and Emily. I am so grateful for your support of my music, and I treasure your friendship.

Of course, I can't forget celebrities like: Vanilla Ice, Perez Hilton, Julio Jones, as well as John Luke, Sadie, Will, and Bella Robertson, who appeared in my videos.

Shout-out to those who have worked so hard behind the scenes on my live concerts, like Mark Weiss and Bret Disend. It is impossible to name everyone who has worked on or behind the scenes of this incredible journey, but you know who you are, and I want to say *thank you*!

Collaborating with lots of different people means learning to work with different personalities. I think I'm pretty easygoing and nice to work with, and most of the time others are, too. You just never know when you might encounter someone who isn't that way, someone who might be a bit more challenging.

Some of the videos will just be Mars and me going out and getting some shots. Other times, it can be a setting in a public place and can have multiple actors on the set. The video for my take on Iggy Azalea's "Fancy" is an example. For that video, we had a bunch of beautiful female models who were filming with me.

I know—it's a tough life, but someone's gotta do it.

We filmed at a boutique clothing store called Dress Up, located in Atlanta. The girls all got to try out different outfits for the storyline.

Fellow singer and friend Brooke Adee sang with me on "Fancy," so she was part of the video, too. With all the people involved, we still didn't take long to get all the shots Mars would need for editing.

Sometimes, filming means sitting around for a long time. You have to wait for everything in the shot to be set up just right. While you're passing the time, you have to stay positive and keep the energy going. That's why we keep things light and have fun. Who knows how long it will take for the director to come up with his big epic vision for what comes next?

One Billion

**A one and nine zeroes, incredible views.
A kid with a dream and an incredible you.
Thank you.**

In the beginning, I just wanted to show everyone how I could rap a song, just like my cousin Marshall was doing. Then my family and some friends would see it, and hopefully they would think it was cool.

That was really it.

Then, by July 2014, I reached the billion-views mark.

One billion.

What can I say to that number?

All I could say, and can say right this very moment, is: THANK YOU!

But even all caps and an exclamation point don't seem like enough. Sometimes I've wondered, *What if I lived in a day and age before YouTube or even the Internet? What if I wanted to perform before rap had ever gone mainstream?*

God puts all of us in the right place at the right time, even when we have no idea that's the case. We don't make things happen on our own. God allows us to make them happen. It can even start

with an annoying seven-year-old wanting to do what his older cousin is doing.

And now . . . who knows what might lie ahead? I hope that all of you who are along for the journey continue to walk with me, wherever this road will lead us.

Part Six

KEEP MOVING AND NEVER STOP, TILL I REACH THE TOP OF HIP-HOP AND POP!

Video Game Chat

If I could go back and talk to myself one day, these are a few of the things I'd say.

Recently seven-year-old me got together with eight-year-old me to discuss video games. My eleven-year-old and twelve-year-old me decided to join in. Here's our conversation.

MB@7: "Club Penguin is awesome."

MB@8: "That's so yesterday. Now all I play is Moshi Monsters."

MB@11: "Hey, guys—listen. I hate to break it to you, but those are pretty silly games."

MB@7: "Making igloos and having parties is fun."

MB@12: "Want to know what's fun? Black Ops."

MB@7 & MB@8: "Black what??"

MB@12: "It's a Call of Duty game. A first-person shooter game."

MB@7: "You're allowed to play it?"

MB@12: "Yep. And you aren't."

MB@11: "I love Madden football."

MB@12: "Yeah, that's awesome. We should play sometime."

MB@8: "Your games don't have pet monsters, do they?"

MB@12: "Black Ops has zombies."

MB@8: "We have—let's see—Poppet and Zommer and Furi."

MB@11: "I remember Poppet!"

MB@7: "I love to meet all sorts of people and just hang out with them."

MB@11: "It's a lot more fun scoring touchdowns. Plus, you never know who you're talking to on Club Penguin or Moshi Monsters."

MB@7: "There are rules. You can get banned if you break them."

MB@12: "That sounds so dangerous."

MB@8: "I love my moshlings."

MB@11: "Oh yeah? You should see my team."

MB@12: "You got killed, what are you talking about?"

MB@11: "No, I'm finally able to recognize man coverage verses zone coverage."

MB@7: "I'd rather be a penguin than a football player."

MB@11: "You're such a baby."

MB@7: "Be quiet, I'm redecorating my igloo! Then I'm going to go out on a secret agent mission."

MB@12: "I'm going on a mission, too. I'm battling against evil on Earth . . ."

MB@11: "That sounds cool."

MB@7: "Not as cool as my rainbow Puffle. And my Puffle Hotel."

MB@8: "My moshlings are way more fun. Look at them. Coolio. Oddie. Scamp."

MB@11: "Turn off those songs. I can't get them out of my mind."

MB@8: "Bongo Colada!"

MB@12: "I still sing that song sometimes!"

ELEVEN-WORD SHORT STORY

Someone said you can't write an eleven-word story. Hmm . . . Debatable!

Collaborations

When you think you've seen it all
and you're at the end,
let me introduce you to my friends.

Hey, guys," Dad said to Mars and me one day. "Look at these sisters. Aren't they adorable?"

My father had discovered a Christmas video of four sisters who were all dancing. Soon, he would reach out to their parents to ask about a possible collaboration.

This was how I ended up working with the Haschak Sisters.

The oldest is Madison, then there's Gracie, Sierra, and Olivia.

Initially we had reached out to them to see if they were interested in being dancers at one of my shows. Then we asked if they wanted to be a part of one of my videos. Then we got them singing on a video. It has just continued with more and more videos and songs. Now my father and Mars are working with them to develop a following and a brand, much like mine.

We've discovered that the Haschak Sisters really do fit with what we're doing now. They're close sisters from a family that shares a lot of our values. The older sisters could be off trying to pursue careers in LA and fitting in with all the other girls their age, but they chose a different path. They're trying to be modest and create content for a mass audience that's family friendly, just like I'm doing.

It's great to find amazing talent and discover that they share the same sort of heart and soul as you do. It's also great to watch singers like the Haschak Sisters being discovered and embraced by YouTube.

The sky's the limit, and finding friends along the way who you can relate to and have fun with and understand . . . that just makes the journey all the better.

Inside Out MattyB

You might dig some of the things I've said.
But let me tell you 'bout **what's in my head.**

Everybody loves Pixar movies—the *Toy Story* films, *Finding Nemo, Cars, WALL-E,* and *Up.* All of them are great. And one of the most recent ones, *Inside Out,* doesn't disappoint. It's fun to see what's happening inside the mind of an eleven-year-old girl.

But . . .

She's eleven, so yes, I can relate. Except . . .

She's a *she.*

The main character is a girl who has Joy, Sadness, Anger, Fear, and Disgust all telling her what to do. Joy and Sadness are the two main characters in the story.

Now, if they had done an *Inside Out* showing my mind, I think I would have added a few other characters. First, I'd want to show my competitive side, and there are two emotions that seem to go with it. There's Pride, which can be a good or bad thing, depending on how proud you might be. And then there's Frustration.

When you're competing, you strive to be the best. When you're winning, you can feel the thrill of what you're doing. But losing . . . I hate losing. I get frustrated and irritated when I'm losing at something.

The other character I'd add would be Goofiness. Yes, Joy can be funny and silly, but Goofiness would take this to a whole new level. Goofiness would make lots of dumb jokes that make no sense. He could make strange sounds or could act like a total moron. Goofiness wouldn't care. He'd just keep laughing, never really thinking of anything else.

Oh, and Hunger.

That's obvious, right?

As a guy, I hear from Hunger a lot more than all the others combined. Or maybe Hunger just has the loudest voice.

Goofiness is making strange noises, while Pride and Frustration are yelling at the game on television, and in between the two is Hunger. He's staring at the bag of chips in front of him and shouting *"Doritos!"* Sadness and Fear would have to sit back on the couch, unable to get a word in edgewise.

Inside MattyB.

I think that would be an awesome movie!

Delivery

Times **are** changing, and things are **rearranging.**

I n the old days, you used to have to buy an entire album of songs. First came records—vinyl. Then there were rectangular plastic cassettes with hundreds of feet of magnetic tape inside them. Along came silver discs called CDs. And now there's digital music, where an iPod can hold a thousand songs.

YouTube showed up after that, and I'm sure glad it did.

If YouTube wasn't around, I'd probably just be a normal kid playing sports and going to school and hanging out with his friends and occasionally stepping up in front of the crowd to showcase some talent. Now I'm that same normal kid, except I'm putting music up online.

Some people ask: "What happens if YouTube disappears?"

It's not something my parents or Mars or I worry about. We've been put in this place, and we continue to take it day by day, seeing what opportunities open up. We watch things evolve and change. I'm evolving and changing, too.

In six years, so much has changed. The appearances we've done and the songs we've recorded and the ways we've filmed videos—we continue to evolve.

Dad and Mars talk about the next few years—when I'm thirteen, fourteen, and fifteen years old—as being defining years for me. Mars says this has been the age when some really big pop stars have separated themselves from the rest of the music world and gone to a whole other level. But you can't *make* those things happen.

All we can do is continue to work hard and walk in faith.

I just don't want to be put into any kind of box. Am I grateful to be considered a YouTuber? Absolutely. But that doesn't define me.

Whether I'm seven or thirteen . . . that doesn't define who I am. Neither does the platform I use to share my music. This is why we continue to try new things out. It's why I keep an updated vlog and why we're collaborating and putting on shows and doing more and more things.

How long will all this last? Great question. But we don't really think about it too much. Maybe five years from now, there will be

another *big thing* that hasn't been launched yet. Just like when YouTube started, or Facebook and Twitter before that.

I just love entertaining and making people smile. No matter what the new platform is, I'll be there so I can announce to the world that there's never been another you or me. No other MattyB, see?

Content Is King

**Want something to do next time you're bored?
Just be yourself, and then press record.**

The traditional model of celebrity is different than it used to be. Someone like Kim Kardashian isn't an actress or a musician, yet she's a celebrity with a huge brand. She provides entertainment, and that is her content.

Mars says that anybody with the ability to create can build a foundation of material. This body of work then can be consumed by others, who will have an opinion on it. So in a lot of ways, it doesn't matter how the content is delivered, whether it's YouTube or Twitter or Facebook or anything else. Some people focus too much on trying to be on every social platform out there. That means you're focused on a wider distribution, when you should be spending your time creating content.

We realize we can't do everything and be everywhere at once. We need to use technology to our advantage. That means continuing to create quality videos for kids my age. I'm sure as I continue to get older, my songs and videos will change, just like my audience.

TWELVE YEARS OLD IS AWESOME BECAUSE:

✦ **You're almost a teen, but you can still eat from the kids' menu**

✦ **You can get free cookies at the grocery store**

✦ **You're still in middle school, so it's not so stressful**

✦ **You can still be silly and play dumb games, and it's okay**

Playing Different Positions

I go after mine after I mastermind.
I can do it, it just takes some time.

I've always loved watching football and playing it with my friends and brothers, but this past year, I really fell in love with playing on a team.

As a quarterback, I can fake a handoff and then sneak out and run to the side. I did this against Blessed Trinity, and I managed to get around a blocker and score a touchdown. I can also spot the wide receiver sprinting down the field and throw the game-winning score. While nothing really beats being a quarterback, there are lots of positions I enjoy playing.

It's fun to play running back, taking the ball and then attempting to slip around the defenders trying to tackle me. Sometimes you just have to plow through everybody. You just rush ahead and don't worry about being slammed to the ground.

I love catching the ball, especially when there's an open field in front of me. Or jumping into the end zone and then doing a little victory dance.

Playing linebacker is fun, because you get to try to *stop* the other team's quarterback. You get to burst through the offensive line and try to sack the QB. Nothing feels better than making a sack on a third-down play, forcing them to punt.

Then there's playing on special teams, catching the ball that's been kicked and then trying to get a touchdown. I've done that, too, running all the way back after fielding a kick.

Right now, I'm loving football and all the different positions I'm playing. It's exhausting, but it's also a thrill.

It reminds me of my music and all the different things I'm doing in it. Being on stage is sorta like being the quarterback. Instead of holding the ball, you're holding the mic, and everybody's watching you. Sometimes I'm brainstorming song ideas like a coach on the sidelines trying to figure out plays. I might be helping with the video shoot, the same way a lineman is digging in and making tackles. Every now and then, I have to do something new and unusual, which is like playing on the special teams.

I'm ready for anything in football, the same way I am in my music. You can never learn too much. Knowledge helps with everything, whether you're in a classroom or on a field or standing on a stage.

Challenges

Don't think that it's all about you.
Sometimes you gotta try something new.

n 2015, Mars's wife, Rebecca, told him about an idea she had for a video.

"Have you seen these challenge videos?" she asked.

"No. I don't have time to know all the latest trends and such."

Rebecca couldn't believe that Mars didn't know about popular challenges out there. "You're overseeing all these brands on YouTube with billions of views, and you don't know what a challenge video is?"

She showed Mars what they were, and so we decided to give it a try. They're really very simple.

One of our big challenge videos was a pizza challenge with Sarah Grace and me.

Okay, okay . . . Sarah Grace is in the video, so yes, we already know it'll be a home run. But let's continue.

In the video, Sarah Grace and I were given the challenge to make our own "special" pizzas. There were ten bags full of very interesting toppings. Each of us had to pick numbers out of our bag and then select the topping.

My toppings consisted of Goldfish, Vienna sausages (gag), marshmallows, sardines (double gag), and gummy bears.

Sarah Grace's toppings were cookies, tuna, pickles, fruit, and popcorn.

My pizza was quite disgusting. One bite, and I had to spit it out.

Sarah Grace won . . . by a landslide. She actually enjoyed her pizza!

So far, we've done every sort of challenge from mystery drinks to Pringles to flavored Oreos and smoothies.

They're crazy, but fun. And Rebecca was right—people love these videos.

It's a great way for people to get to know me, my family, and my friends. It's a little like inviting you over to my house to hang out. Of course, I can't bring a million people over to my backyard, so . . . video blogs like these will have to do.

Maybe one day I'll be doing a vlog showing me jumping out of an airplane or something like that. Wait, my mom just said no to that one.

I think that'd be pretty cool, though. I'll just file that one under "maybe."

Random Things

People are listening, so say something interesting!

Here are some random things I think about.

I like most vegetables, but I don't like beets. Yet my favorite color is red. Weird, right?

Sometimes, I watch a cooking show and think, *I could do that.* Then I wonder how I can get the ingredients to try it out. Maybe I'll make something incredible and go on to be a world-famous chef.

I wonder about my future wife and our children. Who will I be married to, and how will I meet her? How many kids will we have?

What will it be like when my brothers get married? Will their wives all be as cool as Mars's wife, Rebecca? What if one of them hates rap music in general, or even my music specifically?

I wonder if there's some guy out there who is worthy of marrying Sarah Grace. Some guy who would have to earn the approval of my parents and all my brothers, and then after all that, he would have to go through me. (Do you think he's out there? I hope there's someone as amazing as Sarah Grace to stand by her side at the altar one day.)

What will tomorrow bring? What does next year look like? I'm not going to worry about it because it'll take care of itself. I just have to do everything I can today.

Tomorrow is not promised to anybody. Today is all God has given us.

I'm telling you all of this mostly so I can remind myself!

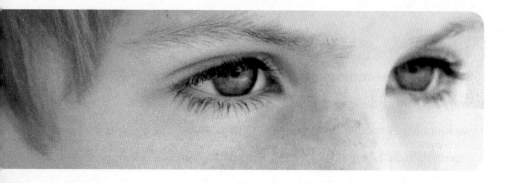

Role Models

**You're somebody who I look up to, it's true.
Show me what you think I should do.**

Do I think the stars of today should be role models for young people looking up to them?

Absolutely.

Here's the thing about being in the spotlight. You have to be the one to step into it. Even if someone helps you get there, you choose whether to stay there or not.

Being in the spotlight is a gift and a privilege, not a right.

More than that, it's an opportunity.

Do people make mistakes? Totally. Should we forgive them when they ask for it and own up to those mistakes? Absolutely.

Some performers say, "I never claimed to be a role model, I never told you to look up to me." But when you perform up on a stage, the audience is *literally looking up to you*. That's the life of a performer, and it's a responsibility you have to accept.

I already know that people look at me differently because of my music and videos. That's okay. I'm cool with that. Can I show them how to be kind to others? How to treat people with respect and show love? How to dream big and try to do something crazy and awesome in your life? How to prevent the haters from bringing you down?

I don't want to just be *in* the lights, I want to *be* a light. I want to show younger kids that, hey, you can be a good guy and make the right decisions. I hope and pray that I do.

It sure helps having people in my life who hope and pray that I do, too.

It has never been easier to find an audience than it is now. So for anybody who's got an audience: show love. Be positive. Have gratitude.

Dad and Mom

**You're the reason that I am who I am,
and you're teaching me the right way to be a man.**

Every day should be Mother's Day and Father's Day.
Seriously.

Now don't think I go around acting like that every day, even though I should. I'll admit that I don't. I'm just like any other kid.

But I do love and appreciate my parents. They've both encouraged me to dream big and to be myself. They also do so many things for me, especially ever since this wild musical journey started.

I wanted to share some of the things I love about my parents. I'll start with Dad.

I love playing games and sports with him. Both the real stuff—baseball and football and basketball—and the video games. My father was once the best player in the country (or maybe the world?) in a golf video game. For real.

Dad always supports the things I want to do, both in music and in sports. Really, in whatever activity I want to pursue. He's careful about my time, and always offers his guidance. That said, he's always willing to give me a chance to pursue something.

He manages my music career and all of its different aspects. Sure, he kind of has to, since I'm so young. But he seems to enjoy doing it, and I'd never have any idea how to do it otherwise.

Maybe the greatest thing about Dad is that he teaches me and our family about God. Faith is the center of our family and everything we do. All the choices my father makes start from our faith.

As for my mother, she also encourages me with my music and sports and various things I want to do. She's always been creative and driven, so she supports the things I'm trying out, too. She encourages me to be anything God says I can be and is supportive when I decide to follow my dreams.

Mom spends most of her time driving me and Sarah Grace and my brothers to our friends' houses and to school and to the various activities we have going on. I'm sure that when Josh and I get driver's licenses, she's going to be very happy. Just like my father, Mom teaches us about God in our youth class at church and by participating at my school as a volunteer. Mom cooks for all of us. She gives me back scratches. She's loving and always there for me.

I'm so grateful for my family and for my parents. All the things I'm doing now—I couldn't do any of that stuff without them.

Guaranteed

It's easy to **focus on you,** **but you never know** **what someone else** **is going through.**

Mars has always told me to make sure I'm *there* when meeting a fan—to never just go through the motions. He says that even though I've been stopped a ton of times and asked if someone could get their picture taken with me, I should never be rude or act like I don't have the time. Even if I've done this hundreds of times before, I shouldn't ever act like it.

For the person asking, this might be their one and only time ever making the request. I have a duty to make them feel special. I need to treat them the same way they treat me. We all have times when we're tired or irritated, and often we take it out on our parents or our siblings. For me, there are a lot more people who are paying attention, so I have to be extra mindful.

That's the message and story behind the song "Guaranteed." It's about dealing with perceptions some people have of me. They want to meet MattyB, someone they might have an image of or their own idea about. When I'm suddenly myself, perhaps being a little more quiet and laid-back, they're wondering what happened.

Sometimes I can walk into a room and feel shy. If I don't speak up and be friendly, people might automatically assume I'm being rude to them.

I'm definitely not trying to be rude. It's something I have to continue to work on and get better at.

Girls can still make me nervous.

Some guys can still be intimidating.

Some grown-ups can be bossy or . . . well, kinda boring to a twelve-year-old.

Sometimes I'm just not very interested in talking, period.

The thing is this—we shouldn't judge people by appearances. Quiet doesn't *always* mean uninterested.

At the same time, we always need to be respectful and giving of our time.

I'm trying to learn to find this balance. As I learn, I'll share my emotions and feelings and questions in my songs.

They're a good place to try and figure out life.

So Much Joy

I wanna take time and tell you that I'm thankful for you.
You're the reason all **of these dreams** are coming true.

I will never forget this moment after a concert at a meet and greet.

It was a typical evening, with a long line of maybe three hundred or four hundred kids. Each one would come up to me and smile and usually seem nervous.

"Hi, what's your name?" I would ask.

"I love your shoes," I might say.

Or, "That's a pretty dress," or else, "Where are you from?"

Maybe, "Have you ever been to my show before?"

It's always fun to meet BGirls and BBoys. The little girls, so shy and looking down and having their parents smile and take pictures. But on this night, after one kid after another came, and I greeted them and gave them a poster, all of a sudden, two parents were standing in front of me.

By themselves. Without a kid.

Both of them were crying and holding a picture in their hands.

Everything sorta stopped. Mars and I got quiet, along with the rest of the meet-and-greet room. Security stopped shuffling people through.

The mother began to talk to me, wiping away her tears. "We just wanted to come and let you know—this was very special for us tonight," she said. "We bought the meet and greet for our son . . . We wanted to tell you thank you ourselves. Our son was eight years old and diagnosed with cancer. He passed away a few weeks ago. We wanted you to know how much joy and strength you brought him. We would sit with him in the bed and sing your songs, and he would listen to them before surgery. He had thirty-nine surgeries before he died."

I didn't know what to say. Neither did Mars. We just stood there amazed, and we tried to hold back the tears in our eyes. These parents had come out to the show just to tell me this about their son. I held the picture and looked at the smiling face. A kid. Just like me.

A kid knowing he's sick and feeling pain and counting his days. And being able to turn on a video we made with the idea of bringing people joy and fun. Listening to the composition Mars and I made, watching my rapping and dancing.

I picture him listening to the song and feeling a little happiness.

Unfortunately, I never got a chance to meet this kid. But at least we connected through the music.

God allowed me the chance to do this thing I love, this thing that makes *me* really happy. And the best part is, it can make others happy, too. Even those who are in pain, who need it most.

I'm humbled. All of us are humbled.

I might question what to do sometimes, but then I simply trust that I'm doing the right thing. My parents and Mars and our family continue to ask God for wisdom. For these moments. For these chances. We certainly think they're divine. Every song has a spirit behind it, and we believe that it's bigger than anything we control.

God does indeed work in mysterious ways.

Let's all give a collective *chyeah* to the awesomeness behind stories like these—and to the awesome God who lets the flowers spring up, even in our darkest hours.

Georgia Dome

I'm not sure what to think of this.
It feels big.
Living this life, but I'm just a kid.

On November 1, 2015, I performed with the Haschak Sisters and Brooke Adee at halftime of the Atlanta Falcons game. Seventy thousand people surrounded me as I stepped onto the field, but I wasn't nervous. Numbers are kinda weird things. My dad and my cousin will share these numbers with me and I'll be like, *that's cool*, not really getting it. But the cheers were loud, and that's the fun part of my job. The stage felt familiar and comfortable. We began to perform, and it just felt right. The audience reaction sounded great.

Earlier that year, I had posted a vlog listing what was on my bucket list. These are the things I had listed:

1. ride a water jet pack

2. ride a shark

3. throw out the opening pitch for a Major League Baseball game

4. perform the halftime show at an NFL game

5. go to Paris with my future wife

So yeah—I'd already managed to get number four done!

Could number five be just around the corner?

Okay, I'm doubting that I'll be getting married anytime soon. But performing at the Falcons game was a dream come true.

Looking Ahead

Forget what you've been told.

I'll make music until I'm old.

I'm excited to turn thirteen. To finally become an official teenager.

Sure, it might be easy to wonder about what's coming down the road. To worry about questions that can come to mind.

What's going to happen after my voice changes?

Well, it's already starting to, and the world hasn't ended, so it's all good.

What kind of music should I be doing next year or the year after that?

All we need to worry about is today.

Will all those people who discovered and loved that seven-year-old kid missing his front teeth continue to follow him with his career?

I hope so. Maybe some won't, but maybe some new people will come along for the ride. The key is trying to capture who I am right now, today.

Lots of people out there try to ride a wave that's already starting to come down. I think what we've always tried to do with the music is find what the market and the culture are talking about and then wrap my brand around it.

But what's your brand, MattyB?

Well, it's just that. MattyB.

Twelve turning thirteen, in the sixth grade. So what does middle school and high school look like? What about college and beyond? What about marriage and a career and children and grandchildren?

Some might be full of questions like that, but I'm happy just trying to see if I can beat Mars in golf this afternoon. The rest will take care of itself.

Videos are a lot like freezing time for a moment, right? Anybody who creates—I guess any artist—shares with others a snapshot of himself, where he's at the moment he's creating.

The future I want to figure out is, when are we going to Yogli Mogli again to get a frozen yogurt?

As for looking back, like I've been doing in this book, I just have to say how awesome it's been. These first twelve chapters of my life have been incredible. I believe that the chapters to come will be even more awesome.

So watch out, world.

Mom and Dad have taught me not to fear, to rely on God, and to know that he has this all worked out. Sometimes, our plans are not his plans. Dad and Mars certainly know a little something about that. But God does wonderful things when we trust him.

For now, I'll just continue enjoying being a kid. Wait—am I a kid? I'll say enjoying being an almost-teenager.

Let's Go

Forever is a long time,
especially since **forever never rewinds.**

Keep following your dreams!"

How many times have I said that? But I've said it to myself even more than to you. The lines I rapped in "Forever and Always" are still true to this day. I know them by heart, and not just because I sing them a lot. I know them because they're *from* my heart.

"Dream what you wanna dream."

Don't let anybody tell you it can't be done. Maybe there are limitations and realities that you have to acknowledge, but a dream is something beyond all of that. A dream allows you to fly to unknown places and do things that can't be done. That's why it's called a dream, because it's wild and crazy, and then you wake up.

Except sometimes you dream big and realize you never went to sleep.

You're living the dream. But first, you had to imagine it.

"Go where you wanna go."

Go off the map to places that can't be mapped. Find places inside yourself, places outside your comfort zone, places that could only ever seem imaginary. Then dream about ways to get there, whether it's a magical location you want to visit in person or an emotional place at which you want to arrive.

"Love who you need to love."

That means everybody. 1 Corinthians 13:13 says this about love: "Three things will last forever—faith, hope, and love—and the greatest of these is love." So love everybody you need to love, and that's *everybody*.

"Know what you wanna know. Think what you're gonna think. Say what you're gonna say. Be who you wanna be."

Know what you can about yourself. Be confident in what you think and what you say. There's only one of you, right? God made you exactly how you are, so embrace it. After that, there's only one thing left to do:

Figure out the person you want to be, and then *be who you wanna be*.

Chyeah.

Thirteen-Plus People
I Need to Thank

First of all I would like to give credit to God for choosing me to be a voice; Mom and Dad; Mars and Rebecca; Sarah Grace and my brothers Blake, John, and Josh, who have been there for me; my grandparents and all my family and all those close to me on the MattyB team. And last but certainly not least, all the millions of B-Family MattyB fans who are the best in the world and have inspired me so much with their loyalty to move forward with my music. Love you all.

Thanks also to Travis Thrasher for helping me with this book, as well as Carolyn Reidy, Louise Burke, Jennifer Bergstrom, Jeremie Ruby-Strauss, Nina Cordes, Becky Prager, and Jennifer Robinson at Gallery Books.